Welcome to *Explodapedia*, the indispensable guide to everything you need to know!
This series is packed with in-depth knowledge you can trust; it gives you the tools you need to understand the science behind the wonders of our world. Read on to discover the story of how we became the way we are, in *Evolution* . . .

'Extraordinary discoveries are explained in this book in a way everyone can understand.'
Sir Paul Nurse, Nobel Prize winner

'The perfect balance between charm, quirkiness and wonder . . . for kids and adults alike.'
Siddhartha Mukherjee, Pulitzer Prize winner

'A totally fascinating book, brimming with amazing scientific knowledge and fab illustrations.' **Greg Jenner**

'Successfully blend[s] appealingly humorous drawings . . . with text that combines clarity and accuracy.'
Professor Richard Fortey

'Both accessible and funny . . . a clever way to introduce . . . our understanding of all life today.'
Professor Venki Ramakrishnan, Nobel Prize winner

BM: To Ghyll, the most up-to-date evolutionary prototype in our family. Keep asking those great questions. x

MA: To Connor and Spencer, thank you for evolving so beautifully.

EXPLODAPEDIA
EVOLUTION
How We Came To Be

Ben Martynoga

Illustrated by Moose Allain

David Fickling Books

Explodapedia: Evolution
is a
DAVID FICKLING BOOK

First published in Great Britain in 2023 by
David Fickling Books,
31 Beaumont Street,
Oxford, OX1 2NP

Text © Ben Martynoga, 2023
Illustrations © Moose Allain, 2023

978-1-78845250-2

1 3 5 7 9 10 8 6 4 2

The right of Ben Martynoga and Moose Allain to be identified as the author and illustrator of this work has been asserted in accordance with the Copyright, Designs and Patents Act 1988.

All rights reserved. No part of this publication may be reproduced, stored in a retrieval system, or transmitted in any form or by any means, electronic, mechanical, photocopying, recording or otherwise, without the prior permission of the publishers.

Papers used by David Fickling Books are from well-managed forests and other responsible sources.

DAVID FICKLING BOOKS Reg. No. 8340307

A CIP catalogue record for this book is available from the British Library.

Printed and bound in Great Britain by Clays, Ltd, Elcograf S.p.A.

Italic type is used in *Explodapedia* to highlight words that are defined in the glossary when they first appear, to show quoted material and the names of published works. Bold type is used for emphasis.

Contents

Consider the Fly	7
Chapter 1: How Evolution Works	17
Chapter 2: Bugs, Birds, Beasts and Bellyaches	30
Chapter 3: Natural Selection	40
Chapter 4: It's in the Genes	53
Chapter 5: The Rise of the Replicating Robots	74
Chapter 6: Why Should Anyone Care?	86
Chapter 7: Seeing the Light	105
Chapter 8: All Kinds of Everything	120
Chapter 9: You're History, Sunshine	137
Is This the End, or the Beginning?	152
Timelines	160
Glossary	163
Index	169
Acknowledgements	172
About the Author and Illustrator	173

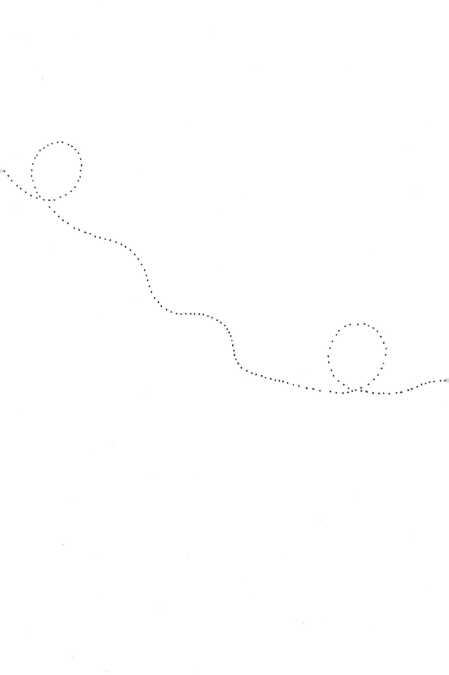

Consider the Fly

What's the point of flies? They're annoying. They buzz. And, of course, they hang out in the most disgusting filth – then come and land smack bang in the middle of your dinner.

Oh, great. Here's a fly now. Get lost!

Not until you apologize.

A **talking** fly?! Go on, zip it, or you're getting squashed.

Never gonna catch me!

OK, OK, you're right. You flies **are** practically impossible to swat. And, actually, what we really want to do is take a closer look at you. Do you mind?

S'pose not. As long as it's only to marvel at my sleek physique.

WHY YOU'LL NEVER CATCH A HOUSEFLY WITH YOUR BARE HAND

First, let's check out those eyes. They might look fairly ordinary at first, but they're actually two compound eyes:

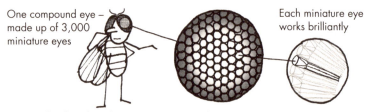

One compound eye – made up of 3,000 miniature eyes

Each miniature eye works brilliantly

That's why flies can see what's going on all around them – and see **you** coming a mile off.

Just like the cells in the *retinas* at the backs of your eyes, cells in a fly's compound eyes contain tiny, highly sensitive detectors made from proteins, which convert light into electricity. When the fly 'sees' something – like a rolled-up newspaper rushing towards it – those electrical signals zip along nerve-*cell* 'wires' and into the brain, which decides what to do about the threat.

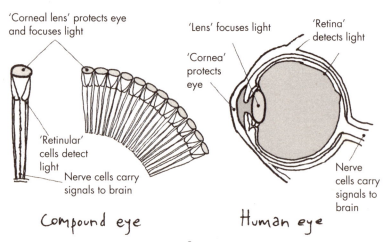

'Corneal lens' protects eye and focuses light

'Retinular' cells detect light

Nerve cells carry signals to brain

'Lens' focuses light

'Cornea' protects eye

'Retina' detects light

Nerve cells carry signals to brain

Compound eye   Human eye

8

But all this happens extremely quickly. Flies process visual information **seven times faster** than you do. From a fly's point of view, each tick of a clock's second hand feels like it takes seven whole seconds. So, to a fly, we humans look like we're moving in slooowwww motion.

And that gives me **ages** to react.

Which is why flies always seem to . . . **fly** off, extremely quickly.

Also, for their size, flies are vastly stronger than we are. Because they have an *exoskeleton*, which basically means a skeleton on the **outside** of their bodies, they can pack more muscle power **inside** their bodies.

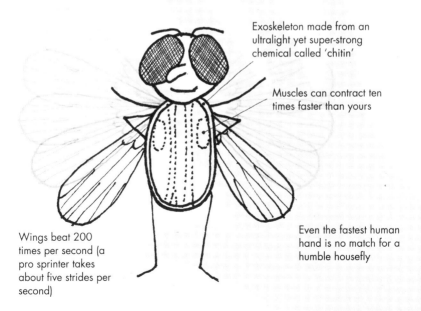

Exoskeleton made from an ultralight yet super-strong chemical called 'chitin'

Muscles can contract ten times faster than yours

Wings beat 200 times per second (a pro sprinter takes about five strides per second)

Even the fastest human hand is no match for a humble housefly

OK, so flies' bodies are awesome, but they're still filthy little creatures.

How dare you! We're always grooming ourselves!

Fair point!

Next time you spot a fly, watch it for a moment. You'll see it wiping itself down with its front legs. Flies rely on their senses. They use chemical sensors embedded in their legs to 'taste' their world – constantly. If they don't keep those sensors, as well as their compound eyes, nice and clean, they'll get lost and confused.

And, actually, it's worth knowing that if flies –

And all our cute little maggot babies.

– didn't join forces with all the other *detritus*-eating beasties that gobble up and recycle dead and decaying waste, that waste would just hang around for ever. And our world would stink a whole lot worse.

So, who, exactly, were you calling pointless?

Maybe that was a little harsh.

Take a proper look at any living thing and you'll find that

it's amazingly well-suited to its surroundings. Its body parts seem tailor-made to do all the work needed to keep it alive and able to multiply itself, whenever it gets a chance.

Think about the grass in your local park that's constantly being mowed, nibbled, scuffed, stomped and peed on. It just keeps on growing back. Incredible, eh? And all it needs to stay alive is a bit of sunlight, the occasional splash of rain and a thin layer of soil.

That soil is even more amazing.

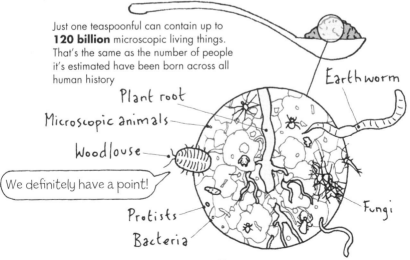

Just one teaspoonful can contain up to **120 billion** microscopic living things. That's the same as the number of people it's estimated have been born across all human history

They absolutely do. These minute underground creatures are utterly crucial. Without them there'd be no soil. And without soil there'd be no plants and, therefore, no plant-eating animals – which means there'd also be no 'us'.

> I'll never take soil for granted again!

If you could peer into the minuscule bodies of those soil *microbes*, your mind would be truly boggled. You'd see thousands of intricate, *molecule*-sized machines, all working away 24/7. Together, they perform the elaborate chemical reactions needed to break down the waste other living things leave behind, keep themselves going and make the fertile soils plants need. Though these microbes are tinier than the smallest specks of dust, their moving parts all look every bit as carefully constructed as the much larger bodies of plants and animals.

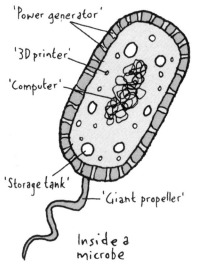

Inside a microbe

Now look in the mirror. Whether or not you like what you see, there's no denying that the human head is fitted with some impressive equipment. Most of us are lucky enough to have a set of hungry sense organs, which are constantly gobbling up information about the world around us.

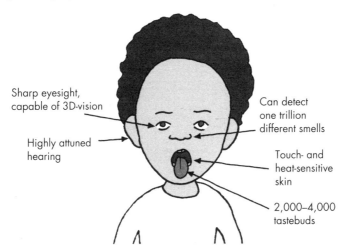

Sharp eyesight, capable of 3D-vision

Can detect one trillion different smells

Highly attuned hearing

Touch- and heat-sensitive skin

2,000–4,000 tastebuds

And in between those ears is a brain that's more than a match for any manmade supercomputer. It uses all that sense information to livestream the most addictive, fully immersive, multi-sensory virtual reality computer game ever. Only it's not virtual reality, it's your actual reality.

You can't fly though, can you, big head?!

OK, so we don't have wings. But that's exactly the point: different bodies are purpose-built for life in different *environments*. It doesn't make any sense to say that some bodies are better than others. And, besides, we don't need wings. Thanks to our brains, we can fly . . . in aeroplanes.

That's a question people have been pondering for as long as they've been able to ponder. We're lucky enough to live in an age where we **know** the answer.

Here's what it boils down to: all living things have been carefully crafted, over aeons of time, by the extraordinary, and often incredibly creative, process we call *evolution*!

THE PLANET-SIZED INNOVATION LAB

Evolution basically means 'gradual change'. So, when we say a living thing has evolved, we mean it is a modified version of a different living thing that existed in the past.

Human being today

Homo habilis: human being's relative two million years ago

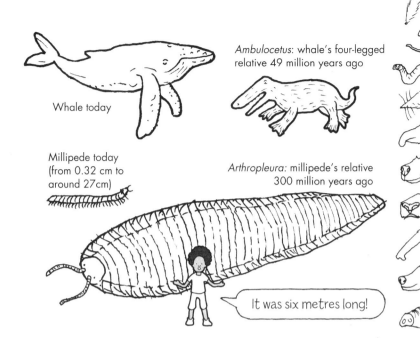

Whale today

Ambulocetus: whale's four-legged relative 49 million years ago

Millipede today (from 0.32 cm to around 27cm)

Arthropleura: millipede's relative 300 million years ago

It was six metres long!

Evolution modifies living things through a never-ending process of 'trial and error'. In each new generation, some *organisms* grow and behave in ways that differ slightly from their parents. Some of these differences make creatures' lives harder. But successful ones produce individuals that are better at surviving and reproducing within their particular surroundings. Over many, many generations, success has built on success, gradually creating all the different creatures that creep, swarm, sprout, spread, ooze, bloom, squawk, flap and buzz across every corner of our planet.

Evolution has been running these 'experiments' for an eye-wateringly massive amount of time. In fact, biologists now know for certain that all *species* around right now are related to the very first **living things** that spluttered into life on our planet back in the deep shadows of time. That means they've **all** been evolving for around **four billion** years!

Life has had its ups and downs, however. On several occasions things got so bad that it was almost **snuffed out** entirely. But some living things have always found a way to persevere and, thanks to evolution, adapt themselves to their new circumstances whenever the world has changed. That's why you can actually think of today's life forms – including you – as the most up-to-date prototypes to have emerged from a planet-sized innovation lab. It's a lab that has been tinkering with its designs, non-stop, for thousands of millions of years.

Hey, there's no improving on **this** design.

We're all works in progress, actually, Fly. Your type of body will gradually be altered. And future flies might even evolve into something that isn't a fly at all. That's evolution for you – everything that's alive is, and always will be, in a state of change. Now, sit tight, because we're about to find out how it actually happens.

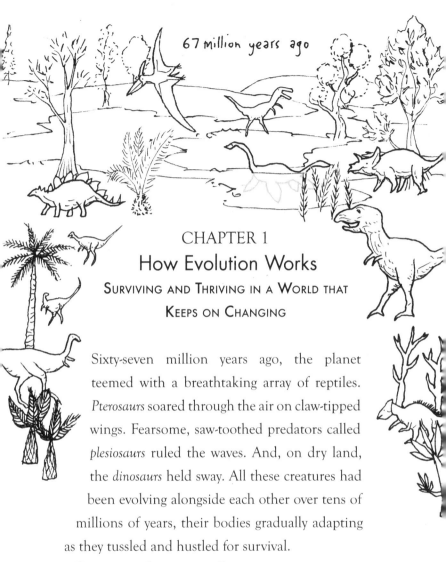

67 million years ago

CHAPTER 1
How Evolution Works
Surviving and Thriving in a World that Keeps on Changing

Sixty-seven million years ago, the planet teemed with a breathtaking array of reptiles. *Pterosaurs* soared through the air on claw-tipped wings. Fearsome, saw-toothed predators called *plesiosaurs* ruled the waves. And, on dry land, the *dinosaurs* held sway. All these creatures had been evolving alongside each other over tens of millions of years, their bodies gradually adapting as they tussled and hustled for survival.

Then, around sixty-six million years ago, a massive, ten-kilometre-wide meteorite slammed into our planet, detonating an explosion with the same energy as **one billion** atomic bombs.

66 million years ago

The seas literally boiled and the shockwave and *megatsunamis* that followed slaughtered dinosaurs and their reptilian cousins in their countless millions. The reign of the giant reptiles came to an abrupt and very messy end.

Some living things managed to survive the hellish blast, but the new world they had to live in was truly abysmal. The oceans turned dangerously acidic and the sun disappeared behind a thick cloud of toxic soot; smoke, dust and blazing hot debris encircled the planet and occasionally rained fire on the creatures below. Plants, seaweeds and *plankton* couldn't properly harness the sun's energy, so Earth's *food chains* collapsed. In total, scientists think three-quarters of all species alive at the time died out completely.

Not one of the pterosaurs or plesiosaurs survived, but the dinosaurs weren't **all** wiped out. A small fraction of them made it through the catastrophe. In fact, they eventually turned one of the greatest natural disasters of all time into an **opportunity**, and they've been evolving ever since. That's the incredible thing about evolution, it means living things can change, generation by generation, and at least stand a fighting chance of coping with whatever nasty surprises the world might throw at them.

Here's one of the dinosaurs whose *ancestors* lived through the utter havoc the meteorite wreaked all those millions of years ago:

Yup, biologists agree that chickens – and all of today's birds – are dinosaurs. Believe it or not, they all evolved from a small, feathered dinosaur that lived around 150 million years ago. By the time the meteorite struck, however, some of its descendants looked much more like today's birds.

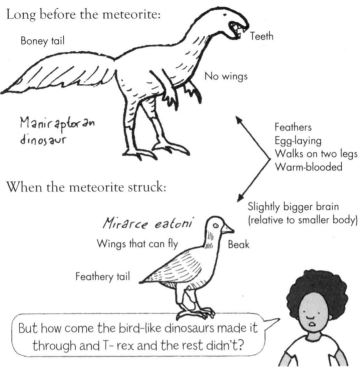

Nobody knows for sure, but even 66 million years ago, birds had evolved a whole range of *characteristics* that biologists think may have saved their skin after the meteorite turned Earth into a living hell:

1. Since most land animals died and the forests had burned down, food was suddenly very scarce. Thanks to their **beaks**, birds could peck at the tough seeds and nuts, pick at carcasses and gouge grubs out of decaying wood.

2. Birds were **smaller** than most other dinosaurs. They needed

less food and would have found it easier to hide when trouble loomed.

3. **Wings** were great for getting out of trouble and searching for better places to live.*

4. Compared to their body size, bird **brains** are generally **bigger** than reptile brains, and therefore better at solving problems and remembering where to find food, etc.

They evolved them, through an awesomely powerful process called *natural selection.* That's what built the dinosaurs' incredible bodies – and what turned some of them into birds.

The basic idea of natural selection is pretty straightforward: in a population of living things, individual organisms vary, and the ones that happen to be best at surviving and *reproducing* ... survive and reproduce more than all the others.

The ways in which individuals vary are usually quite small and subtle. Just think about your family, or your neighbours. They're all people, obviously. But they have different eyes, hair, skin, facial features and so on – because they're all **individuals.**

* Though some scientists think the birds that survived the meteorite were not able to fly.

That's how it is for all living things: every organism is an individual.

Biologists call the small differences that distinguish one individual from another *variations*. If a variation proves even a tiny bit helpful when it comes to surviving and reproducing – and if it gets passed on to the next generation – it might combine with other variations to trigger more dramatic evolutionary changes. That's how it must have been for some of the maniraptoran dinosaurs, way back at the start of the birds' evolutionary journey. Some of them will have had snouts that were just a tiny bit 'beak-like', arms that were slightly 'wing-like' and so on. And, crucially, those little variations must have given them some kind of advantage.

> But if the variations were so tiny, how could they **possibly** lead to massive changes like whole sets of actual wings?

Because lots and lots of little changes over a huge amount of time **add up** to truly monumental changes. In fact, that chicken we met earlier can show us how it works.

Over the centuries, chicken farmers have bred all sorts of different varieties of hen:

How did they do it? They used something called *artificial selection*. It works just like natural selection, except humans do the selecting instead of nature. So, in order to make a chicken with a giant pompom of feathers on its head, the breeders found a hen and a cockerel with slightly fluffier-than-average head feathers and encouraged them to mate. Then, when the chicks grew up, they picked out the ones with the fluffiest heads and got **them** to mate. From one generation to the next the changes would have been small. But over many generations they definitely added up . . .

> All that effort just to make a hen look stupid!

That's a matter of opinion. What's not up for debate is the fact that artificial selection is a kind of evolution. A powerful one.

> So, could you use it to turn a chicken back into a T-rex?

Ha! It might not work, but you could definitely try. By choosing to breed hens and cockerels that look and act the most 'dinosaury', and carrying on breeding them over tens of thousands of years (you'd need the help of many future relatives), enough tiny changes **could** mount up and eventually morph an ordinary chicken into a far more terrifying beast. It wouldn't be a T-rex, but it might look a bit like one:

Nature Does the Designing

In artificial selection, **people** push evolution down a particular path to 'design' living things with characteristics that are useful to humans.

But in the wild the **same basic process** works without anyone doing any 'designing' or 'selecting' whatsoever. Nature does that job for itself. That way populations of living things are constantly adapting themselves to their environments and following their **own** evolutionary paths. Just like the one that transformed small, feathery dinosaurs into today's birds.

Yeah, yeah, dinosaurs turned into birds through natural selection, yawn. Bet you can't explain how it works though.

We can, actually. The fact is, it's not just a process that happened in the past to make dinosaurs, birds, mammals and us, it's happening all around us, all the time. And while it usually takes ages for natural selection to make really big changes, scientists can sometimes see it happening much more quickly . . .

LATCH ON LITTLE LIZARD!

In September 2017 the Turks and Caicos Islands in the Caribbean were battered by two ferocious hurricanes, one after the other. Waves taller than the average house crashed ashore, winds reached 265 kilometres per hour and thousands of trees and bushes were ripped from the ground. It was a terrible time for all the islanders, including the small anole lizards that called those uprooted trees 'home'.

A month after the hurricanes, a small team of lizard-loving biologists flew to the islands to check up on the reptiles. They'd measured the bodies of lots of anole lizards **before** the storms, and were amazed to discover that the hurricanes seemed to have changed their proportions. The average survivor lizard had slightly **longer** front legs and slightly **bigger** toe pads. Of course, the storms couldn't actually have triggered the sudden growth of these body parts. Instead, the biologists realized they had just witnessed natural selection in action. The lizards that survived the hurricane were the ones that had been able to cling on for dear life - they had been naturally selected. Most of the lizards with shorter front legs and smaller toes had died.

What's more, the changes were permanent. Eighteen months later, the survivors' offspring still had longer front legs and bigger toes. They had *inherited* the characteristics that had saved their parents.

If the hurricanes keep getting stronger or strike more often - and most scientists think they will, because of the *climate crisis* - the anole lizards will go through many more rounds

of intense natural selection. Hopefully, they'll evolve an even better grip and all sorts of other characteristics to help them survive extreme weather events.

THE RACE THAT NEVER ENDS

Natural selection doesn't just kick in after a natural disaster, like a giant meteorite or a hurricane. It's actually at work in all living populations, all the time. Any individual organism with a set of inherited characteristics that gives it an edge has the potential to pass those characteristics on to its offspring. The offspring will benefit from the same features – e.g., by living longer and reproducing more – and pass them on to **their** offspring. Eventually, the most successful characteristics will spread through the whole population.

> It's like some sort of competition!

Yes, where the winners end up making more winners. But evolution by natural selection is a competition that **never ends,** because:

1. The environments organisms live in keep changing. For example, when food runs short, space gets tight, a new predator or disease arrives on the scene, floods happen, droughts strike or the planet's entire climate changes.

2. The organisms, or competitors, keep changing. With each new generation there's always a chance that some individuals will be born with completely new characteristics that no one in their parents' generation shared.

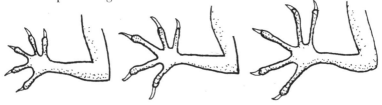

One day an anole lizard could be born with extra-long claws. As well as hanging on in the strongest winds it might gain new skills, such as the ability to hunt (and eat) bigger prey

But what have lousy lizards got to do with how I evolved my incredible body?

OK, that's where the mind-bendingly huge spans of time come in. Thanks to millions of years of natural selection, flies like you evolved from creeping bugs that looked like this:

Ugh. It doesn't even have any wings!

Exactly. Natural selection may take **ages** to build fancy structures like wings, and it never has a particular end goal in mind, but give it enough time and it can achieve some truly extraordinary things.

Step by minuscule step, natural selection built Fly's amazing wings. Over millions of generations it turned some of the descendants of sharp-toothed, wingless dinosaurs into sharp-beaked birds with working wings.

And, dear reader, the same gradual and painstaking process even wired up **your** amazing brain – and without that, you definitely wouldn't be able to understand evolution.

The helpful 'inventions' that natural selection comes up with, such as lizards' gripping toes, birds' beaks, flies' wings and the circuits in your brain that allow you to read, are called *adaptations*. With each new generation, it's the creatures with the adaptations best suited to life in a particular place, at a particular time, that produce more offspring than the rest. In short, natural selection makes sure the winners keep winning and making more winners.

Now, pack your bags, grab your butterfly nets and your seasickness tablets. We're about to hop back two centuries to join the legendary Charles Darwin – the person who figured out the theory of evolution by natural selection – on a genuine voyage of discovery.

CHAPTER 2
Bugs, Birds, Beasts and Bellyaches
THE VOYAGE THAT CHANGED BIOLOGY FOR EVER

It's 27th December 1831, in the port of Plymouth, England, and a 22-year-old scientist called Charles Darwin has just walked up the gangplank to board a sailing ship, HMS *Beagle*.

Darwin isn't actually a trained scientist at this point. Having dropped out of medical school (he couldn't stand the sight of blood), he then started studying *theology* at Cambridge University, so he's really just a part-trained vicar. Throughout his student years, however, he'd been far more fascinated by the wildlife thriving in the **outside** world than by the stuff he was learning **inside** his college. Deep down, he knew he wanted to be a professional biologist, but that wasn't really a job in the 1830s.

Darwin was resigned to keeping biology as a hobby, until an unbelievable opportunity came his way. One of his college professors, who'd noticed Darwin's passion for natural history, put him forward for a position that would change his life for ever. He wouldn't be paid, and the post was only temporary, for two years (which turned into five!), but it did mean Darwin could focus on biology 24/7 and set about turning himself into one of the most brilliant scientific minds of all time.

As he steps aboard the ship now, Darwin's new role is just beginning.

Let's meet the ship's captain, Robert FitzRoy.

The HMS *Beagle*'s mission is to make detailed surveys along the coast of South America. FitzRoy and his crew plan to focus on the **non-living** geography. It is only at the last minute that the captain thinks about bringing someone along to study **living** things too.

Young Darwin has no particular goal in mind and FitzRoy says he can do pretty much whatever he pleases.

But, as they set off across the Atlantic Ocean, Darwin struggles to find his sea legs.

Between bouts of seasickness Darwin does a lot of reading and thinking.

At this time, lots of people in Europe and beyond still believe the Christian story of creation is basically correct. According to the Bible, God had created the world and all living things over the course of one highly productive week. In the 17th century, Archbishop James Ussher had even worked out that this crucial work must have been completed less than 6,000 years earlier, at precisely 6 p.m. on Saturday 22nd October 4004 BCE!

At the start of his journey, Darwin believes that God is indeed responsible for bringing life into existence, but like many of his contemporaries, he doesn't think all the details of the Bible stories are **literally** true. In particular, Darwin has serious doubts about the precise timing of events. These doubts are confirmed by a book he's reading as the *Beagle* lurches its way across the ocean.

The book is by a *geologist* called Charles Lyell, and it contains a huge amount of evidence that starts to convince Darwin that Earth **has** to be far, far more than 6,000 years old. According to Lyell, it might be thousands of millions of years old. Even more shockingly, Lyell's book says that landscapes aren't solid and fixed for ever. They are in fact always changing. Everyday forces that seem so simple – like the constant drip, drip, drip of water, or the build-up of mud and sand on a seashore – can, over huge stretches of time, completely resculpt entire environments, even carving whole valleys and mountain ranges.

This thought plants a tiny seed in Darwin's mind that will, in time, grow into a truly massive idea.

> If the Earth itself is always changing, mustn't living things have some way of changing and adapting themselves too?

After two months, the little sailing ship finally makes it to South America. Desperate to get his feet back on dry land, Darwin leaps ashore and does what most 19th-century nature-lovers like doing best: he goes hunting. He wants examples of all the exotic living wonders he encounters and sets about catching them with gusto.

In Brazil, Darwin is dazzled by spectacular rainforests. Hungry to learn about all the world's creatures, he enjoys watching monkeys, spotted tree frogs and rainbow-feathered birds dancing through the jungle canopy. He's just as delighted by creepy-crawlies that he finds down at ground level, though their behaviour sometimes horrifies him:

Darwin will be haunted by these wasps for the rest of his life.

Further down the coast of South America, Darwin finds the *fossilized* bones of some massive, deeply unfamiliar creatures. They make him think of the discoveries made by an English *palaeontologist* called Mary Anning, earlier in the 19th century.

Mary Anning

The huge fossilized skeletons of marine reptiles she'd found and studied had sent shockwaves through the scientific world. At a time when science was dominated by rich men, Anning, a woman from a poor family, turned herself into an expert on collecting and interpreting the fossils of *extinct* animals. Her discoveries helped prove that there had once been an 'age of reptiles'. They forced scientists and religious leaders to ask some awkward questions, such as: If God made all animals, why don't dinosaurs appear in the Bible? And, if God didn't create dinosaurs, where had they come from and what had become of them?

The giant fossilized beasts Darwin finds aren't dinosaurs, however, they're mammals.

Darwin also finds the remains of a gargantuan llama, an armadillo as big as a car and an elephant-sized sloth. The monsters obviously died long ago, but they get him thinking about how one kind of creature might slowly change into something quite different.

> Could these giants be the long-dead **relatives** of today's much smaller sloths, armadillos and llamas?

On a trek into the high Andes mountains he finds fossilized sea creatures, and this finally convinces him that Lyell is right: the planet is ancient and constantly changing.

> If these mountains were once part of the seabed, what forces could possibly have raised them up to this lofty height?

Soon enough, Darwin gets some answers. First, he watches in awe as a volcano erupts, spewing out lava that then solidifies into brand-new rock. Then, in Chile, he sees the effects of a massive earthquake, which rearranged the landscape before his very eyes...

> If a single earthquake can do this, how much must things change over **millions of years**!

Seabed now 1.5 metres above high tide mark

Live mussels   Seaweed

Four years after leaving England, the expedition reaches a cluster of volcanic islands poking out of the Pacific Ocean, about 1,000 kilometres to the west of Ecuador. They're called the Galápagos Islands. As soon as he ventures ashore, Darwin is assaulted by the aggressive heat of the climate. He finds the rugged, lava-strewn landscape strange and sinister, but is immediately awed by the bizarre creatures that live here:

That's a very good point, Fly. There are more insects in the world than any other kind of animal. But compared to the South American mainland, only a small number of insect species live on the Galápagos. Darwin notices this, and it triggers a fresh flurry of ideas . . .

Insects have fragile wings. Few could survive the 1,000-kilometre flight from the mainland.

Have all the bizarre animals and plants on the islands always been here? Or did they arrive from elsewhere and then adapt to life on the edge of a volcano? And how did there come to be so much variety crammed onto one small group of islands?

Among the many plants and animals Darwin collects are a series of drab-looking brown birds. He's intrigued by their beaks. A bit like the various blades on a Swiss army knife, they help each kind of bird to eat a different type of food.

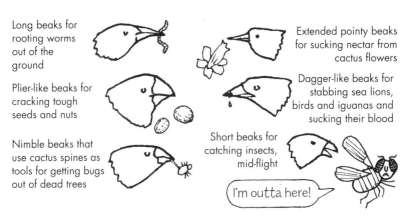

After five weeks of frenzied collecting, the overloaded *Beagle* leaves the Galápagos Islands and ploughs onwards. It crosses the Pacific to New Zealand, skirts beneath Australia, traverses the Indian Ocean, rounds the Horn of Africa, cuts back across to Brazil and, finally, returns to England in October 1836.

Darwin heads home with a vast treasure trove of specimens and his mind churning with new ideas. By now he is convinced that planet Earth is almost unimaginably ancient. He also understands that it's in a state of constant change. He isn't quite ready to abandon the belief that God created all living things, but he's pretty sure that species themselves can evolve.

Living things **must** be able to change. If they'd been designed once, long ago, they'd no longer match their surroundings today.

But **how** did life evolve? That's the puzzle Darwin brings home with him, the one that he's now absolutely determined to solve.

CHAPTER 3
Natural Selection
'THE SINGLE BEST IDEA THAT ANYONE HAS EVER HAD'

Darwin was not the first person to argue that living things evolve over time. In fact, his own grandfather, the doctor and poet Erasmus Darwin, had floated a similar idea 15 years before Darwin was even born.

At around the same time, a French scientist called Jean-Baptiste Lamarck had hatched another theory and, in 1809, published a long book in which he did his best to figure out how evolution worked.

Darwin read everything that his grandfather and Lamarck had written, but he was not very impressed.

A few years after his return to England, that's precisely what Darwin himself came up with. He devised a brand-new way of truly understanding evolution: his theory of evolution by natural selection.

On his voyage, as well as a fine set of whiskers, Darwin had accumulated more specimens than even the hardest-working biologist could ever dream of studying in a lifetime. He needed help sorting through this mammoth mountain of evidence and, luckily for him, lots of other scientists were desperate to get their hands on his unique collection of tropical creatures.

Among them was a famous ornithologist called John Gould. Darwin had assumed that the birds he'd found on the Galápagos Islands (see p. 39) were completely unrelated; their beaks just looked too different. 'Nonsense,' said Gould, the birds were all different kinds of finch.

Gould's surprising insight helped Darwin focus on the question that perplexed him most:

Darwin called this 'the mystery of mysteries', and over the following months he uncovered a series of new clues that would let him finally get to the bottom of it.

A Recipe for Change

Key to Darwin's big breakthrough was his realization that living things have four crucial properties which, when combined, mean they will **always** evolve by natural selection. We can think of it as a recipe with four essential ingredients:

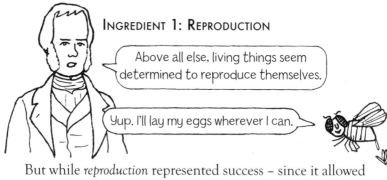

But while *reproduction* represented success – since it allowed organisms to make sure their kind continued to exist into the future – Darwin saw that it also caused many of life's biggest problems. That was the message he took in 1838 from a depressing book written 40 years earlier by a man called Thomas Malthus. Malthus argued that whenever the human population got too big, disaster – in the shape of famine, disease and war – would always follow, bringing the population crashing back down.* Darwin realized that the same must apply to all living things.

> Life is a **constant struggle**. More individuals of each species are born than can possibly survive.

Ingredient 2: Variations

We've seen how people use artificial selection to breed chickens (see p. 23) and all kinds of other domesticated plants and animals. In Victorian England, breeding pigeons was a popular hobby. Darwin was one of the first people to truly see this as a kind of evolution. He focused on the key fact that:

> Individual pigeons are different. The breeder just exaggerates natural variations that already exist.

Curly feathers

Turned into:

Very curly feathers

---

*Thanks to new medicines, farming techniques, clean water systems, etc., the human population is now far bigger than Malthus ever thought possible.

INGREDIENT 3: HARDSHIP

One spring, Darwin's wife's vegetable patch suffered an unusually late frost. Most plants in a row of beans were killed, but some survived and went on to grow beans. Perhaps they had shoots that could withstand icy temperatures better? This showed Darwin that even invisible variations can have **life-or-death consequences** and how variations can become useful adaptations (see p. 29).

INGREDIENT 4: FAMILY RESEMBLANCE

Just like his father and his grandfather before him, Darwin had a big nose, an occasional stammer and a hatred of alcoholic drinks. These characteristics seemed to run in his family. Darwin realized the same must be true of the more obviously helpful adaptations that are 'naturally selected' in all living things – e.g., a powerful grip in anole lizards (see p. 26) or improved vision in houseflies (see p. 8).

Evolution **only works** if offspring inherit the adaptations that helped their parents survive and reproduce.

In 1839, Darwin suddenly realized how to blend these four ingredients to explain how natural selection worked.

Darwin's New History of Life

Thanks to his new theory, Darwin had a way of seeing – in his mind's eye – events that actually played out over millions of years. And that meant he could finally explain how **one** species of finch could turn into **many** different species of finch.

Here's roughly how he thought this history **might** have unfolded:

4 million years ago Massive undersea volcanic eruptions form the largest of today's Galápagos Islands.

3 million years ago Over the years different living things swim, drift, fly, wash, wriggle and crawl ashore. Gradually, all kinds of life forms start to flourish on the new land.

2 million years ago One monsoon season, a freak storm blows a small flock of finches, all of the same species, over from the South American mainland. On the Galápagos, there's plenty of food and no predators. It's party time for these lucky finches. They get reproducing (Ingredient 1 – see page 42), and their population booms.

1,999,990 years ago With finches hatching everywhere, suddenly there isn't so much food to go round. Then a series of droughts kills their favourite food plants. Life is suddenly much tougher. It's every finch for itself in what Darwin called the 'Struggle for Existence'.

1,999,989 years ago By chance, a finch hatches with an unusually large beak (Ingredient 2 – see page 43). This variation means it can crack seeds that are too tough for the other birds. It survives the drought just fine (Ingredient 3 – see page 44), pairs up with another survivor and they get breeding.

1,999,988 years ago Their babies inherit their family's big beak characteristic and the same appetite for seeds (Ingredient 4 – see page 44). They grow up and reproduce too. Big beaks become more common among the finch population and new variations appear and are selected, making beaks even bigger.

1,999,000 years ago Over many generations, the descendants of the original finches – which had stubby beaks for eating fruits and insects – gradually acquire a powerful new adaptation: a plier-like, nut-cracking beak. This new population of big-beaked finches has evolved, via natural selection, into a distinct species.

Around 190 years ago Darwin visits the Galápagos. The 'plier-beaked' finches are still going strong. This population is still evolving, but slowly – natural selection had come up with a successful design, and there's been no need to make any big changes since.

Whenever life got tough, or finches entered a new environment by hopping from one island to the next, birds born with slightly different beak shapes found they could feed themselves – and avoid competition with other finches – by adapting their diet. Small variations gradually got bigger and, eventually, different groups of evolving finches were so distinct that they became different species. Today, there are 18 species of finch on the Galápagos – each has evolved a unique set of adaptations that tailor them to a particular lifestyle. What's more, biologists now think Darwin was 100% right: they all evolved from one original ancestor species.

Darwin's theory of natural selection did far more than describe how one kind of little brown bird could change into another. It solved the other massive puzzle that had been troubling him for years:

Now I see how **all living** things can adapt themselves and keep going whenever their worlds change!

But there was even more to it than that. Darwin quickly realized that if different species of finch could be connected together by chains of relatedness, **every species** could be connected to every other species too. Later on, he explained it like this:

All the organic beings which have ever lived on this earth have descended from some one primordial form.

What he meant was this: all organisms, including us, can trace their ancestors back to the **very first living things**. Every species alive today is, therefore, a tiny twig on the same vast family tree. Even flies and humans are cousins.

Really? Next you'll be saying I'm related to this banana.

You are, Fly! We all are.

TOO BUSY TO CHANGE THE WORLD?

In 1995, a philosopher called Daniel Dennett described the theory of evolution by natural selection as *'the single best idea that anyone has ever had'*. So, once he'd hatched his brave new idea, you'd imagine Darwin couldn't wait to share it . . . Did he scream 'Eureka!' and run through the streets explaining the secret of life to everyone in earshot?

Nope. That definitely wasn't Mr Darwin's style. Instead, he described the basics of natural selection to a few friends and then sat on it . . . for nearly twenty years.

Some people say he was afraid. After all, he lived in a much more religious age, and was saying that God didn't necessarily have a part in the story of life's creation. That was pretty shocking.

But today most experts think there was a better explanation. They say he delayed because he was an extremely thorough scientist: he wanted to think through all possible criticisms and make his theory bomb-proof. Plus, his health wasn't great, he was busy with his growing family (he had ten children and, for a Victorian gentleman, was an unusually engaged dad) . . . and then there were his barnacles.

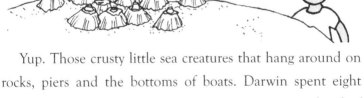

Yup. Those crusty little sea creatures that hang around on rocks, piers and the bottoms of boats. Darwin spent eight years, from 1846 to 1854, scrutinizing every minute detail of their lives in order to confirm his new theory.

Enter Genius Number Two

Darwin knew natural selection was monumentally important, and he fully intended to write it up and share it with the world.

He just hadn't quite got round to it.

That suddenly changed in June 1858, when he received a letter from a young naturalist called Alfred Russel Wallace. Like Darwin, Wallace had been on an expedition to the tropics, to collect and study all kinds of plants and animals. Like Darwin, Wallace had digested a huge amount of evidence and come up with a nearly identical theory for how species evolve.

Darwin was impressed by Wallace's insights, but didn't want the younger scientist to publish his ideas first and claim all the glory. In the end, Darwin and Wallace agreed to share the credit, by having their ideas announced together, at a meeting of scientists in London, in July 1858.

By that point, many of the scientists in the room had already accepted the idea that living things could evolve and, at the meeting, barely an eyebrow was raised. Somehow, the audience completely failed to notice that Darwin's and Wallace's new theory explained how the living world worked and would, before long, revolutionize biology for ever.

Undeterred, Darwin set to work, writing about his grand theory in a book called *On the Origin of Species by Means of Natural Selection, or the Preservation of Favoured Races in the Struggle for Life*. It was published in November 1859 and despite its less than catchy title (today it's usually shortened to *The Origin of Species*), every single one of the 1,250 copies printed sold out on day one.

THE MARMITE THEORY: LOVE IT OR HATE IT

Darwin wrote just one line about human evolution in *The Origin of Species*. He simply says: '*light will be thrown on the origin of man and his history*'.

Nevertheless, lots of readers were appalled by this single sentence. Why? Because, if the theory of natural selection was right, there was no longer any reason to think of humankind as superior to any other species. Many people jumped to the obvious conclusion: humans were just a bunch of apes, descended from somewhat different apes, who lived a long time ago. For many, this thought was simply too ghastly to contemplate.

Others absolutely loved the book. The idea that we must have evolved from other *primates* made perfect sense. What's more, it opened the door to an entirely new way of understanding every species under the sun, from aardvarks, *bacteria* and cacti to xemes,* yeasts and zebras.

*A xeme is a kind of seagull.

And as for Darwin himself, he shot off into orbit as one of the greatest scientific superstars of all time.

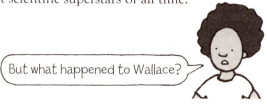

But what happened to Wallace?

Well, his ideas matched Darwin's perfectly, but, amazingly, he didn't seem to begrudge Darwin his success at all. He selflessly said:

Mr Darwin has given the world a new science, and his name should stand above that of every philosopher of ancient or modern times. The force of admiration can no further go!

So he wasn't jealous at all?

Nope. He was just happy to have helped hatch the big idea that explains so much about the living world.

But, as we're about to see, there was still a lot of work to be done before all biologists would fully accept the theory of natural selection.

CHAPTER 4
It's in the Genes
THE PUZZLE'S MISSING PIECE

Darwin's theory of natural selection explained a lot about **why** most living things are so well matched to their surroundings and **how** they adapt when those surroundings change. But right up to the end of Darwin's life, in 1882, and for several decades beyond, his theory suffered from one fatal flaw.

The problem was *inheritance* – in other words, understanding how parents pass characteristics on to their offspring. In his 'recipe' for natural selection (see p. 42), Darwin was clear that 'family resemblances' **and** 'variations' are **both** essential aspects of inheritance. But they're actually complete **opposites**.

• Family resemblances make offspring the **same** as their parents. Partly, this is about making sure helpful adaptations – like the anole lizards' hurricane-proof grip (see p. 26) – get passed on to their offspring. But, it's also about making sure those lizard parents passed on all the instructions needed to build an actual fully functioning living lizard.

On the other hand:

• Variations make offspring **different** from their parents – this explains why some anoles were born with the unusually strong grip needed to survive unusually strong hurricanes in the first place. Variations also explain the many differences in the way you have looked and acted ever since you were a baby, compared to your close relatives.

The same AND different? Isn't that totally impossible?

Nope. That's exactly how inheritance works in biology. But living things have to walk a bit of a tightrope.

With too many 'differences' new organisms don't get built properly. Eventually, they will stop working and die.

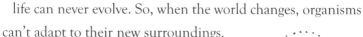

With too much 'sameness' life can never evolve. So, when the world changes, organisms can't adapt to their new surroundings.

Darwin understood all this, but he still couldn't figure out how inheritance actually happened.

How Ducks DIDN'T Get Their Webbed Feet

Back in the early 1800s, the French biologist Jean-Baptiste Lamarck (see p. 40) thought he'd worked out how inheritance balanced the 'sameness' and 'difference' needed for evolution. He argued that offspring tended to be built in the same way as their parents, but animals could create **differences** through the **efforts** they made to adapt themselves to their surroundings.

According to Lamarck, the effort the first ducks put in to swimming gradually stretched the skin between their toes and that change was then inherited by their offspring. Darwin wasn't too sure about some of Lamarck's ideas on evolution, but he thought there might be something in this. It did have an obvious problem, however:

Body builders, for example, don't give birth to amazingly muscular babies.

In the late 19th and early 20th centuries several scientists set out to test Lamarck's theory. Among them was fast-thinking Thomas Hunt Morgan, a biology professor from Columbia University, New York. He thought Lamarck's idea was nonsense, and he wasn't ready to accept Darwin's theory of natural selection either, seeing as it didn't explain inheritance. Morgan had a hunch that flies might be able to provide the missing piece to Darwin's puzzle.

Ahem. The same flies you were so rude about at the start of the book?

It was actually your smaller, less zippy relatives: fruit flies.

See? Flies rule.

Only when they're working with brilliant scientists like Morgan.

Fruit flies rattle through the generations and raise a new brood every 12 days. So Morgan thought that watching them might be a bit like watching animal evolution running on fast-forward. Plus they're really easy to look after: all they need is some glass bottles and a bit of over-ripe fruit.

Thanks to my flies, I can test Lamarck's theory, once and for all.

The experiment was simple: he kept a bunch of flies in pitch darkness 24 hours a day, seven days a week for 19.5 months (the equivalent of 1,400 human years!) and raised 49 consecutive generations.

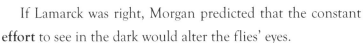

If Lamarck was right, Morgan predicted that the constant **effort** to see in the dark would alter the flies' eyes.

When the flies were eventually allowed back into the light...

Lamarck was right to argue that living things evolved. But he was wrong about **how** it happened: the appearance of new, inheritable variations had nothing to do with a creature's actions.

But Morgan knew he needed a better explanation for inheritance. Over the next three decades, Morgan, his biologist wife, Lilian Vaughan Morgan, and a group of close colleagues, conducted thousands of ingenious fruit-fly experiments. They made three crucial discoveries that started to reveal precisely how inheritance leads to offspring that really are the same **and** different.

Discovery 1: Differences (aka New Variations) Can Appear Out of the Blue

Morgan's next breakthrough happened without anyone – scientist or fly – having to make much effort at all. It showed him that inherited differences, i.e., the variations needed for natural selection, can sometimes crop up randomly, as if from nowhere.

Fruit flies have **red** eyes. But one day Morgan noticed that a fly (that hadn't been raised in the dark) had hatched with **white** eyes, despite having two red-eyed parents.

What had changed to trigger the switch in eye colour? Morgan and his team were about to find out.

Discovery 2: Inherited Characteristics Are Controlled by Genes that Usually Stay the SAME

When Morgan took his new white-eyed fly and mated it with a red-eyed fly, all their children had red eyes.

Intriguing. The white eyes have disappeared.

But it turned out that the white-eye characteristic hadn't actually vanished. When the scientists mated those red-eyed babies with each other, some of the flies in the **next** generation had white eyes!

Whatever it was that **caused** white eyes hadn't changed – its effect had just been hidden.

Wait a minute. This reminds me of something.

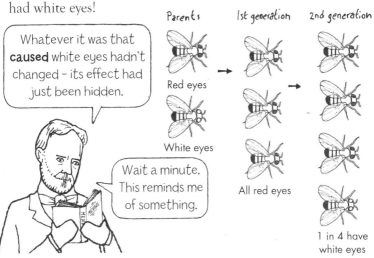

Back in the 1860s, a scientist and monk called Gregor Mendel had done a series of clever breeding experiments,*

---

* For the full story of Mendel's breakthroughs see *Explodapedia: The Gene*.

cross-pollinating thousands of pea plants. He had worked out that all the different characteristics of his pea plants – height, flower colour, pod shape, etc. – were controlled by **instructions**, passed on during reproduction, that tell the next generation of plants how to grow. Mendel called these instructions 'elements'. They came in different variations (e.g., they might make flowers purple or white), and though they didn't usually change from one generation to the next, their effects could sometimes be **hidden**.

Mendel's elements had been renamed *genes* early in the 1900s. But until Morgan and his flies came along, no one had definitively proved that they existed.

Morgan's gene controlled eye colour and came in two variations: red and white. In the years that followed, Morgan's team pinpointed dozens more genes, each of which affected different aspects of flies' bodies and behaviours. And, just as

Mendel had predicted, they all came in different variations. Finally, Morgan was convinced that Darwin's natural selection could work.

Genes were clearly of vital importance, but what kind of 'thing' were they?

Discovery 3: Genes Are Carried on Chromosomes

By the time Morgan started his fly experiments, scientists had proved that **all** living things, from bacteria to blue whales, were made from tiny blobs of living matter called **cells**. Biologists had also noticed that almost all cells contained minute structures called *chromosomes*, which, through a powerful microscope, looked like little threads. In 1902-3 two biologists, Walter Sutton and Theodor Boveri, had suggested that chromosomes might contain the genes.

And, partly because flies are such dribbly little creatures, Morgan and his colleagues had a way to find out.

Flies have no teeth, so they use their saliva to dissolve their food before sucking it up

Sure we make a lot of spit - 'cos we digest our food **before** we eat it.

The cells that produce flies' saliva have chromosomes that are hundreds of times thicker than the chromosomes of other cells, so Morgan's team could see them much more clearly.

The researchers then bred flies that contained different combinations of genes. And they noticed that when the genes changed, their chromosomes changed too:

Fly with White Eye Gene

Each chromosome had a unique pattern of stripes and bulges – a bit like a barcode.

Fly with Crumpled Wing Gene

Fly with Black Body Gene

The only reasonable explanation was that Sutton and Boveri were right.

Chromosomes **do** carry the genes!

Proving that genes were solid, physical objects – i.e., parts of chromosomes – was a massive step forward. It meant scientists could really get down to work, looking at chromosomes inside living cells, picking them apart and running chemical tests to find out how life's most crucial instructions could be contained in these wriggly little threads. And, ultimately, understand why they often stay the **same**, but sometimes throw up new **differences**. From the 1940s onwards the discoveries came thick and fast.

GENE SCIENCE – A CRASH COURSE

To get to grips with evolution, it helps to have a clear idea of how genes work. This crash course on the key 20th-century breakthroughs in gene science explains the basics.

1. Genes are made of DNA[*] A *DNA* molecule is a long chain made up of pairs of 'building blocks', called *nucleotides* (see page 65-6), joined together side by side.

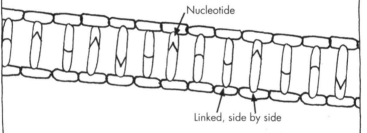

DNA chains coil up into a spiralling shape called a 'double helix'.

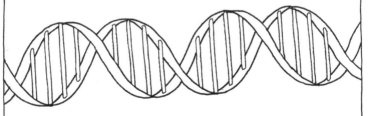

---

[*]DNA is short for deoxyribonucleic acid. Apart from the genes of some *viruses*, which are made from a related substance called *RNA*, all genes are made from it. For full details, see *Explodapedia: The Gene*

2. Chromosomes are massive DNA molecules containing lots of genes Each chromosome is built from a single, unbroken chain of DNA, made from as many as 250 million nucleotide pairs

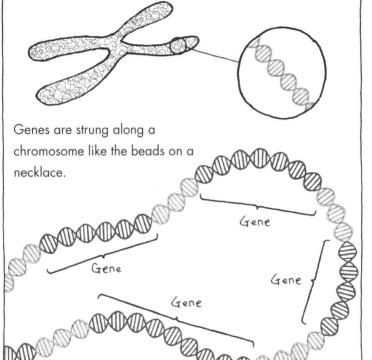

Genes are strung along a chromosome like the beads on a necklace.

Each gene is a block of hundreds to thousands of nucleotides.

A chromosome can contain anywhere between a dozen and several thousand genes.

3. Genes contain coded <u>instructions</u> needed to build and operate living things They're written in a **language** that has a four-letter alphabet representing the four different nucleotides – A, T, C and G.
The information in genes is spelled out in the order in which the four DNA letters appear along DNA's strands.

For a cell . . . **ATTACATGC**
and
TTCGCAGGG have very different meanings

The language of genes, called the *genetic code*, is universal: all living things – bacteria, flies, humans – use exactly the same alphabet, in an almost identical way.

4. The information genes contain is used to make molecules that 'do stuff' Each gene spells out instructions for making molecules of *ribonucleic acid* (RNA) and/or *protein*. Each RNA or protein does a particular job for a cell or body. Together, proteins and RNAs build all living structures and control all the thousands of different chemical processes that keep living things going.

This is a protein called 'haemoglobin'. It carries oxygen round your body inside your red blood cells

66

5. The total set of <u>genes</u> an organism needs is called its <u>*genome*</u>
Some bacteria have just a few hundred genes; most animals have many more:

What?! You lot have more genes than me...?

Human genome:
Genes: ~40,000
DNA letters: 6 billion
Chromosomes: 46

Housefly genome:
Genes: ~30,000
DNA letters: ~700 million
Chromosomes: 12

6. Cells can only be made by existing cells
New cells are made when existing cells split in half, turning one cell into two – a process called *cell division*. Before dividing, a cell **must** make an accurate copy of its entire genome and insert one full copy into both newly formed cells – they need those instructions in order to survive.

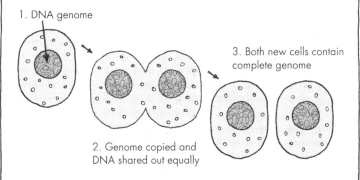

1. DNA genome
2. Genome copied and DNA shared out equally
3. Both new cells contain complete genome

7. Reproduction Reproduction is about getting genes into the next generation of bodies. Lots of living creatures, including most microbes, live their entire lives as single cells. For them, regular cell division is reproduction.

Yeast cells that raise bread usually reproduce by cell division

But for larger living things – most animals (like us) and many plants, whose bodies are made from lots of cells – while the basic aim is the same, the actual process is more convoluted. It's called *sexual reproduction*.

Many flowers and most animals use sexual reproduction

8. Sexual Reproduction

Egg

Sperm

To make a new individual, a male *sex cell* (e.g., a sperm cell in animals, a pollen cell in plants) has to fertilize a female egg cell. Male and female sex cells each contain half the full set of genes, so a *fertilized* egg cell has the full set of genes needed to kickstart a new life.

An entire baby grows because this single cell divides, again and again, to make **trillions** of cells. Cells in different organs have the **same** genome, but they use the instructions it carries in **different** ways.

Er . . . No! Human scientists spent decades doing millions of experiments with all kinds of living things – bacteria, viruses, yeasts, worms, frogs, mice, moulds, cress plants, humans and more – to figure it all out. And we've still got loads of blanks to fill in.

The Differences that Drive Evolution

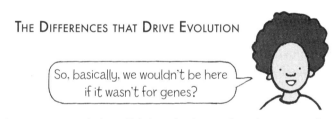

Nope! Genes are vital for all life, which is why it's essential that genes stay pretty much the **same** from one generation to the next. If inherited characteristics kept on changing, new generations of organisms wouldn't have the instructions they needed to grow and survive.

But, as we already know, evolution by natural selection needs differences to choose between – specifically, the **genetic differences** that cause **variations**. So where do they come from?

Except for identical twins, everyone in the world inherits a slightly different set of genes. Even if they share the same parents.

That's partly because genes get **shuffled** up during sexual reproduction. Different siblings each inherit a random mix of gene variations from their (biological) mum and dad.

But brand new genetic differences can also appear suddenly, as if from nowhere.

Exactly. They're called mutations and they happen for two main reasons:

1. **Mistakes** Cells must copy their DNA before they divide. Human cells do this brilliantly, making, on average, one mistake per ten billion DNA letters copied!

2. **Accidents** Certain chemicals (e.g., those in cigarette smoke and engine exhaust fumes), some kinds of radiation (e.g., too much exposure to X-rays or ultraviolet light from the sun)

and some kinds of virus can damage DNA,[*] or change the instructions it contains. Cells have lots of fancy machinery for spotting new mutations and putting them right. But things don't always go to plan, which is why almost every new generation of living thing is born with a genome that contains at least a smattering of brand-new mutations.

MUTATIONS THAT HARM AND MUTATIONS THAT HELP

Mutations sometimes cause problems. For example, cancer and all kinds of inherited diseases, such as *cystic fibrosis* (which mainly affects lung cells) and *sickle-cell disease* (which affects red blood cells), are caused by mutations that stop cells and organs working properly. But they're not all bad news.

Helpful mutations occasionally pop up too. Like the ones that gave some anole lizards the ability to cling on to trees while being hammered by a hurricane (see p. 26).

On the other hand, lots of *mutations* don't make any difference at all. Biologists call them *neutral mutations* because the effects they have don't influence the course of natural selection.

Ultimately, however, the word 'mutation' just means 'difference' or 'change'. It's not for scientists to decide whether a mutation is 'good', 'bad' or 'neutral'. That's up to natural selection.

[*] This includes viruses that infected our non-human ancestors millions of years ago – their DNA is now part of your genome.

Imagine a new gene mutation that alters an animal's stomach cells so it can digest particularly tough leaves. It might be really 'good' mutation for a *herbivore*:

But the same mutation might be 'neutral' or even 'bad', for a *carnivore*. It could make digesting meat more difficult.

A mutation can only be said to have a 'good' effect if it helps individuals, on average, to survive longer and produce more offspring.

Dancing the Natural Selection Two-Step

Mutations are totally random and their effects are unpredictable and risky, but they're absolutely crucial for evolution by natural selection, because it is always a two-step process:

Step 1. Mutations must happen first. They are the original source of the variations that make individuals **individual**.

Step 2. Natural selection kicks in and ruthlessly sorts the mutations that cause helpful variations from those that cause harm.

Since all evolution relies on random mutations, every single one of the amazingly useful adaptations that have been created by natural selection – from a fly's wings to the grey matter inside your skull and everything in between – started out as errors and mishaps. These are the mutations that built up over the generations, gradually forming the adaptations that gave each of your ancestors an edge in their struggle for existence.

In short, life depends on an inheritance system that is extremely brilliant at keeping the crucial information needed to build organisms the **same** from one generation to the next. But because evolution is fuelled by **differences**, there's no way life would still exist today if it never made any mistakes. In fact, without mistakes it couldn't have got started in the first place, as we're about to find out.

CHAPTER 5
The Rise of the Replicating Robots
THE SELFISH GENES THAT RUN OUR WORLD

All organisms, including you, are basically bundles of extremely complicated, joined-up *chemical reactions* – i.e., tiny particles of matter bumping together and making or breaking the *chemical bonds* that link atoms and molecules. Chemical reactions let you digest your breakfast, flex your muscles, heal cuts and bruises, grow your hair and even think.

The special combinations of chemical reactions that do all the amazing things that we call 'life' haven't always existed. They've been evolving their capabilities gradually, across the whole span of Earth's history. So our human story actually starts at the very beginning of it all, long before life itself existed.

Around 4.6 billion years ago, when our planet was brand new, the world's non-living matter had already started going through a kind of chemistry-based evolution. Some scientists have called it the 'survival of the stable'. The rules were simple. They revolved around the basic fact that the chemical molecules that become more common are the ones that:

A) **Are the most long-lived** Think of boulders. They hang around because the molecules inside them are stable chemicals – they can put up with 'wear and tear' and they don't change by immediately joining chemical reactions with water, air or other solid matter that surround them. **Or**

B) **Get created faster than they disappear** Think of *hydrothermal vents*. These are cracks in the seabed where scorching hot rock – normally buried in parts of the Earth's mantle where there is no water – suddenly gets exposed to the sea. When this happens, the molecules in water and mantle rock react violently, producing various gases and a lot of heat. There's an endless supply of rock and water, so the reactions just keep bubbling away. Even if substances made in these reactions float off, dissolve or break down, they build up if they get made faster than they disappear.

Plume of gas

Seawater

Crust

Mantle rock

For the first half billion years of Earth's existence, that was basically all there was to evolution: the main substances on dry land, in the seas and in the air, were made from molecules that were quickly produced or lasted longest. Over the aeons, continents formed, the planet's tectonic plates shifted, and oceans came and went, but overall things changed very, very slowly.

The First Stirrings of Life

Then, around four billion years ago, a new kind of molecule appeared that changed the rules of evolution for ever – some scientists think these were the tiny seeds that all of today's life has grown from. They call these upstart molecules 'replicators', because they had an extraordinary new power: they could copy themselves. Scientists think these replicators were probably based on chains of linked carbon atoms that came into being within a hydrothermal vent.

Here's how they might have worked:

1. The first replicator was a long molecule, built when smaller chemical 'building blocks' bonded to form a chain.

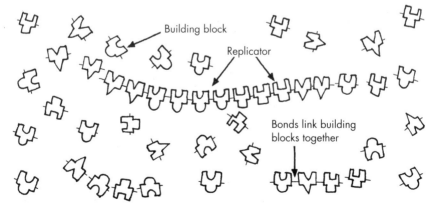

2. Spontaneously occuring reactions in the hydrothermal vent produced:

- A steady supply of new building blocks.
- The energy needed to drive further chemical reactions.

3. The existing replicator worked like a mould for making a duplicate molecule of itself.

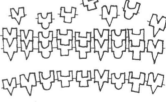

Each building block was attracted to another building block in the replicator's chain

4. Each new replicator molecule went on to copy itself.

Building blocks made chemical bonds with their neighbours, creating a new chain

5. With a supply of new building blocks, replicators could keep copying themselves.

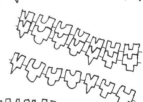

But, inevitably, mistakes happened. Replicators with slightly different chemical shapes and chemical 'likes' and 'dislikes' appeared. Occasionally, mistakes led to replicators that could copy themselves faster or more accurately than the rest.

If we had to pinpoint a moment when life really got started, this might have been it. Suddenly, all four ingredients needed for full-blown natural selection (see pp. 42-4) were in place: replicators **reproduced**. Mistakes, which were basically 'mutations' (see p. 70), meant replicators came in different **variations**. Replicators and their 'offspring' had **family resemblances**. And the harsh conditions of the vent meant they would certainly have faced **hardship**. Inevitably, some replicators fared better than others.

Before long, the cracks and pores in the rocks around the vent were **filling up** with replicators. They jostled for space and battled it out for the resources they needed to replicate themselves. Over millennia, natural selection made sure that

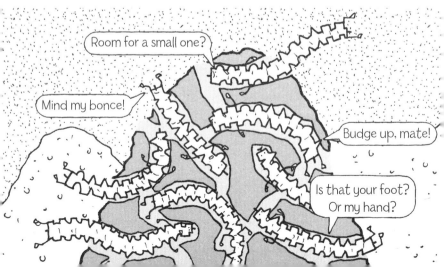

winning replicators kept winning and making more winners. In short, the replicators evolved and set off on the long journey that eventually led to life as we know it.

This is sounding strangely familiar...

Yup. They were behaving a bit like the DNA molecules that form genes today. Some scientists think the first replicators were made from RNA (DNA's chemical cousin – see p.66), which can sometimes replicate itself. What's more, they reckon some of the descendants of the first replicators are still going strong today! At some point they started making themselves from DNA, instead of RNA, and eventually they evolved into the genes that sustain every other kind of living thing in the whole world – including you.

That's amazing!

Yes, it is. But nobody can be 100% sure that the rise of the replicators* actually happened this way. In fact, the various scientists who investigate the origins of life will probably each tell you a different story. Though all their stories will, almost certainly, contain the same two vital elements:

1. **Genes** are essential for all living things, so any believable

*See *Explodapedia: The Cell* for more on the origin of life.

account of the rise of life on Earth needs to explain how they might have come into being.

2. **Natural selection** is the most powerful way – maybe the **only** way – we have of explaining how simple chemicals can evolve into highly complicated chemicals, such as replicators. And how they evolved into the genes that organize the complicated bundles of chemical activity that we call living things.

But how the heck **did** replicators turn into genes?

The big difference between the first replicators and today's genes is that DNA genes have evolved a second crucial function. The first replicators probably copied themselves directly, but genes do it in a less direct way: they contain instructions for making other kinds of molecule from RNA and protein (see pp. 64–8). These molecules are the 'workers' that keep cells alive and copy the DNA when cells reproduce. No one knows when or how replicators started working this way. But, guided by the theory of natural selection, we can **imagine** the next chapters of the replicators' story:

1. As well as copying themselves, some replicators started working as templates for making other substances that could do useful 'jobs' such as:

- Helping replicators attack other replicators and steal their building blocks, so they could grow faster.
- Building defensive shells to protect replicators – the first versions of the *membranes* that surround and protect all cells today.

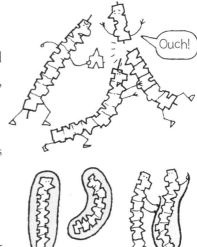

2. Later, groups of replicator-turned-genes started working together, helping to build one another more quickly, for example. Individual genes did best by becoming **team players**. These teams became the world's first genomes (see p. 67), i.e., sets of genes that lived together and co-operated for the benefit of all.

And this 'just happened' by **chance**?!

It does all sound a bit unlikely that simple chemicals just started crashing together and reacting, and then eventually ended up doing all this fancy stuff. But it's not impossible. It's extremely **unlikely**, for example, that you'll win next week's lottery jackpot. Imagine you lived for a million years, though, and bought ten lottery tickets every week. Then you'd be extremely **likely** to win the jackpot at some point. And time was not an issue in the replicators' story – it unfolded over **millions** of years.

But natural selection isn't just about chance. Sure, the events that caused the mutations were **random**, but once those mutations had happened, the process of deciding which variations were winners was often **not random** at all: some genes were simply better replicators. What's more, the 'wins' kept adding up – so genes and teams of genes gradually got bigger and more capable. Their chance of winning the survival and reproduction 'lottery' steadily improved.

> Got it. So when did genes start making cells?

Well, at some unknown point between 3.5 and four billion years ago, teams of co-operating genes must have grown so big and so capable that they could build, control and reproduce entire **cells** – the world's first microbes. Though these cells were minuscule, they multiplied in such gargantuan swarms that their effects on the world were truly colossal. Time and again microbes transformed the chemical make-up of the planet's oceans, its atmosphere and its geology.[*]

Eventually, around 600 million years ago, cells started to band together to form *multicellular* bodies. The first of these were pretty basic and shapeless – a bit like today's sea sponges

[*] For more details see *Explodapedia: The Cell.*

– but gradually they started to develop different tissues and organs. After that, the door was opened for the evolution of all the incredible and often extremely complex bodies of plants, animals and *fungi* (more on this in Chapters 7, 8 and 9). And all that has happened in just the last sixth of Earth's history.

Throughout life's story, the replicators that then turned into genes were always at the very centre of the action:

• Genes contain the indispensable information organisms need to construct their bodies and keep them alive.

• The information in genes **must** be passed on to each new generation.

• Mutations in genes are the main things that trigger the changes in living bodies that we recognize as evolution.

This way of thinking about evolution is called the *'gene-centred'* view. Many biologists think it's the best way of understanding evolution.

SELFISH GENES

In 1976, a scientist called Richard Dawkins published a book called *The Selfish Gene*, in which he says:

> We are survival machines – robot vehicles blindly programmed to preserve the selfish molecules known as genes.

According to the *gene-centred view*, a living body is a temporary robotic vehicle that the genes build, control and drive around for a while, before instructing it to assemble a brand-new robot (i.e., reproduce). But what did Dawkins actually mean when he called genes **selfish**?

Darwin had sometimes described natural selection as the 'survival of the fittest' – which does make evolution sound like a load of self-centred individuals fighting a never-ending series of battles.*

---

* What Darwin was actually saying was that the individuals who 'fit' their environments are more likely to succeed.

But Dawkins knew that individual genes can't actually be 'selfish' – they're just mindless molecules of DNA. All he meant was that the genes that are still around today are the ones that have proved they'll do whatever it takes to get themselves copied again and again, for generation after generation. Sometimes the best way to do that is by building bodies that are only interested in their own survival and reproduction. But sometimes so-called selfish genes do best by working together to build extremely **unselfish** bodies, as we're about to find out.

CHAPTER 6
Why Should Anyone Care?
When Selfish Genes Get Generous

Pyotr Kropotkin wasn't just a scientist, he was also a writer, explorer, political activist and member of one of Russia's richest and most powerful families. As a young man, he'd read and admired Darwin's *On the Origin of Species*, but he hated the way people seemed to be using the 'survival of the fittest' concept to justify the terrible inequality of life in 19th-century Europe.

Kropotkin was so appalled by inequality that he'd launched a campaign for a political revolution – and ended up in prison as a result!

A group of loyal friends felt the world needed to hear Kropotkin's ideas, and they'd risked possible execution to help him stage a daring escape.

The selflessness of Kropotkin's friends got him thinking. Did natural selection automatically lead to a world filled with selfish creatures, locked in a non-stop struggle for supremacy?

Exploring *Siberia*, long before his jail sentence, Kropotkin had observed how living things of the same species didn't waste time and energy **competing**; they survived the brutal arctic conditions of northern Russia by **co-operating**:

In 1902, Kropotkin published a book, called *Mutual Aid*, that shocked many other biologists by arguing:

> *The species in which peace and mutual support are the rule prosper, while the unsociable species decay.*

Kropotkin was convinced that the world's **most successful** animal species weren't the fiercest, the toughest or even the most intelligent. They were the ones that were best at working together.

Extremely Unselfish Ants

According to Kropotkin's studies, no creatures have achieved so much by working together as ants have.

• There are an estimated ten million billion ants alive right now. That's more than a million ants for every human being!

• They live on every continent and in every habitat, apart from the very highest, coldest places.

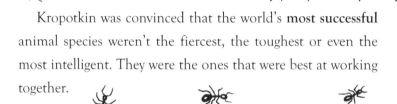

> Their success can only be explained by co-operation!

Ants are *social insects*. They live in highly organized colonies, and will do **anything** – including battling to the death – to keep their colony going. For example:

Army ants use their own bodies to build massive bridges.

An ant colony works like a single living body, constantly sensing the world and making collective decisions about how to get food or fight off threats.

But perhaps most incredible of all is the way most individual ants seem to break the number one rule of natural selection . . .

. . . because most workers in an ant colony **never** reproduce. Usually, all the eggs are laid by a single female queen, while the workers devote their lives to satisfying her every need.

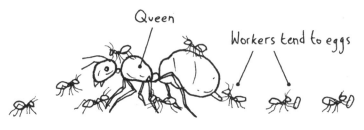

Thousands of other species of social insect – such as bees, wasps and *termites* – give up their chance to reproduce individually too.

If natural selection really was all about rewarding the **individual organisms** that are best at reproducing, worker insects that never breed shouldn't really have evolved. The genes inside these workers' bodies look as if they've reached a dead end in their evolutionary journey.

> I'd say their genes are **stupid**, not **selfish**!

Well, it does seem like strange behaviour. Neither Kropotkin nor Darwin managed to come up with a totally convincing explanation. But, in the 1960s, biologists, including several of Richard Dawkins's (see p. 84) colleagues at the University of Oxford, finally got to the bottom of the mystery. They reckoned that:

> Sometimes helping genes that live inside **different** bodies gives a particular gene its best chance of succeeding.

Bill Hamilton   George Price   John Maynard Smith

That's not as mind-boggling as it sounds. The more closely related a family member is, the more likely they are to share copies of the **same** genes. A gene can 'choose' to make more copies of itself either by:

1. Making the organism it lives in focus on having its **own** children.
2. Making the organism it lives in help its **close relatives** have more children.

Here's how that might work for a single female worker ant:

Option 1. Going it Alone Female worker ant mates with a male 'drone', then struggles on her own to raise a family.

If worker lays 100 eggs – only **8** make it to adulthood:

Total extra copies of each of her genes in the world = **4** (offspring only inherit half of their genes from mum)

Option 2. Putting Family First Female worker ant co-operates with 1,000 other workers to help the queen raise her offspring, so more ants from the new generation survive.

If queen lays 100 eggs – 80 survive to adulthood:

The queen is the worker's mum, so the new ants are her **sisters** – on average, they share half of her genes

Total extra copies of each of the worker's genes in the world = **40**

Still think the ants' genes are 'stupid' for making ants co-operate, Fly?

Well...

Nope. Didn't think so. To an individual gene, the particular body it happens to exist in is irrelevant. So if a gene makes an ant willing to sacrifice its life for the good of the colony, it can still be an evolutionary success. The ant might die, but many copies of the gene that triggers selfless behaviour will live on in its relatives' bodies.

Biologists call the kind of natural selection that made social insects so co-operative '*kin selection*'. It helps explain why so many animals do so much to help their families.

You Vomit in My Mouth, and I'll Vomit in Yours

What kin selection can't explain is the way so many types of creature help completely unrelated members of their own species, without seeming to expect any immediate payback.

The only thing vampire bats eat is the blood of other mammals.

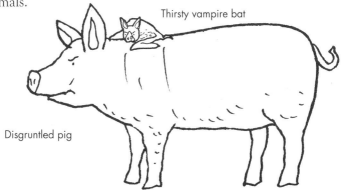

Nowadays, biologists call this reciprocal altruism ('reciprocal' means taking turns to pay back and 'altruism' means helping others without expecting thanks/payment).

When Different Species Join Forces

Across life's history, radically different kinds of organism have evolved alongside one another. Other living things are often the **most important factors** driving evolution by natural selection. After all, unlike the rain or rocks, other organisms can suddenly pop up and try to eat you, or give you a nasty disease. Or perhaps you can try to eat them! Sometimes, however, **completely different** kinds of living thing end up spending their whole lives **sharing** with each other. Biologists today call this *mutualism*, and if mutualism didn't happen, our world would be unrecognizable.

The land wouldn't be green, for a start – **90% of all plants wouldn't be able to grow**! Why? Because almost all plants develop mutualistic relationships with the invisible tendrils of fungi that weave themselves into and around their roots. These fungi are called *mycorrhiza* ('myco' means fungus, and 'rhiza' means roots).

Plants need their mycorrhiza, but the mycorrhiza also need their plants:

Mycorrhiza

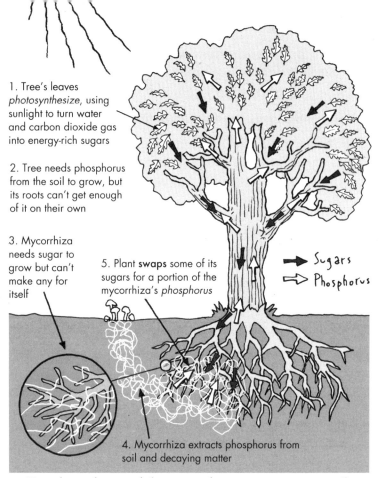

Together, plant and fungus make an awesome team. Over millennia, they've covered most of the available land on our planet with a ready source of food: the plant matter that keeps so many other living things alive.

Without mutualism, the oceans would be radically different too. Coral reefs are some of the busiest and most diverse ecosystems on the planet. If it wasn't for one particularly productive partnership, they'd collapse:

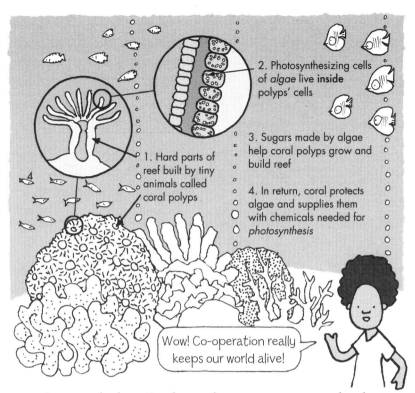

It certainly does. But living things sometimes need to be a little bit suspicious . . .

Beware Cheats and Freeloaders!

Co-operation can bring massive benefits. But relying totally on other living things can also be risky. What if your partner suddenly stopped co-operating, and turned into what biologists call a '**cheat**'?

A mycorrhizal fungus might develop a mutation that means it takes sugars from its neighbouring trees, but keeps phosphorus for its **own** growth.

A vampire bat might take food from its pals, without bothering to feed them in return.

A worker ant's genetic variations might program it to lay its **own** eggs, **while** its queen still creates thousands of siblings.

Individual living things that bend the rules like this get the benefits of co-operation without paying all the costs; they have more time and energy to reproduce **themselves**. But what if the gene variations that trigger these self-centred behaviours became more common?

Luckily, nature has evolved ways of cracking down on the cheats.

How to Beat the Cheats

1. **Families stick together** Living things usually **can** trust that the individuals they live closest to really are members of their own family – and therefore worth helping. This is even true for microscopic bacteria. Because they grow by one cell dividing

again and again to form a clump, any microbe that finds itself in a packed crowd of **similar** microbes is probably surrounded by close kin. For some species, that means it's OK to start co-operating – e.g., by working together to build a *biofilm* that protects the entire clump of cells and keeps would-be cheat species out.

2. **Memory and family resemblances** Vampire bats spend a lot of time grooming one another. It helps them to recognize individuals and remember who has – and who hasn't – shared blood meals in the past. Any bat that takes and never gives will soon find that the others refuse to feed it – until it starts sharing again.

3. **Negotiating** Recently it's been discovered that trees and their mycorrhizal fungi haggle with each other, like traders at a market. They each want what the other has to offer, but they've evolved ways to 'hold back' their precious resources until they can agree a 'fair price'.*

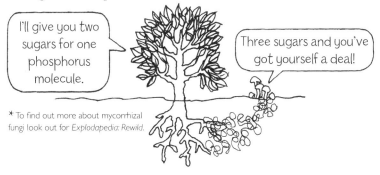

* To find out more about mycorrhizal fungi look out for *Explodapedia: Rewild*.

4. Policing Many ant colonies have evolved ways for workers to 'sniff out' eggs that haven't been laid by the queen and destroy them – often along with the would-be cheat.

Kropotkin **wanted** to believe that co-operation always wins. But his prediction that *'unsociable species decay'* hasn't really stood the test of time.

For instance, *parasites* are living things that have flourished through 'cheating'. They just take, take, take and never give.

When the Parasites Prevail

From the single-celled organisms that cause *malaria* to the mistletoe plants that steal water and nutrients from trees, parasites are basically everywhere.

And if you're a cockroach, you really don't want to bump into an emerald cockroach wasp. Here's why:

1. A wasp stings a cockroach, temporarily paralysing it.

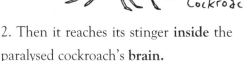

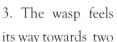

2. Then it reaches its stinger **inside** the paralysed cockroach's **brain.**

3. The wasp feels its way towards two specific parts of the brain and delivers a second kind of poison.

4. The cockroach's escape *reflexes* shut down. Unable to move itself, the cockroach becomes the wasp's **zombie puppet**.

5. Using the cockroach's antennae, the wasp steers its victim into a burrow.

6. Then it lays an egg between the cockroach's legs.

7. The egg hatches and the larva burrows inside the cockroach. The larva spends eight days chewing its way through the organs of the cockroach's still-living body.

8. The cockroach eventually dies. The wasp forms a *pupa*.

9. The adult wasp hatches and goes cockroach hunting.

> That's incredible. But also deeply evil!

That was Darwin's first thought when he watched those parasitic wasps feasting on living caterpillars in Brazil (see p. 34). It pushed him to wonder whether struggle and competition might be the main themes of life's story.

On the other hand, Kropotkin saw geese flocking together and ants collaborating and he jumped to the opposite conclusion. He thought success in evolution was all about mutual aid and co-operation.

But we can't really apply our human ideals of 'right and wrong' to the rest of the living world. Thanks to evolution, emerald cockroach wasps and co-operating ants have each just stumbled across a successful way of surviving and reproducing.

OK, I get that. But where do we humans fit in to all this?

Robots that Care

In some ways, we're just like any other animal: we've evolved in a world that's crammed full of other living things, including other human beings. The interactions we've had with all these different creatures have shaped us. Our evolved instincts sometimes push us towards more co-operation, and sometimes towards competition.

But in other ways, we truly are different from all other animals. We've evolved unusually powerful brains that **can** pause and reflect on the consequences of our actions. That means we really can behave in ways that are genuinely kind. And, most importantly, we can look at the big picture and understand that everything we humans have achieved has been based on our ability to work together. That's been true since our species, *Homo sapiens*, first evolved – around 300,000 years ago – and it's still true today.

No single person could possibly build themselves a new smartphone – or even something as simple as a pencil – from scratch. Most people would struggle to feed themselves if the local supermarket closed unexpectedly . . . The fact is, we need each other. As Kropotkin said, across human history, more often than not, co-operation really has trumped competition.

How? Well, we humans use all of the 'anti-cheat' methods you've just read about (see pp. 98–102). Some biologists actually think the main reason we evolved our powerful brains was to get better at recognizing and punishing cheats. But if that was the only reason, why have our brains also evolved the power of empathy? When we see other people suffering pain and distress, we very often **feel** their pain ourselves. Perhaps those are the feelings that truly motivate us to help.

> That surely helps explain why my dear friends risked everything to save me!

It's not just **our** lives that have been made possible by co-operation. The benefits unlocked by genes, cells and organisms 'deciding' to work together have steered the evolution of life since its very beginnings. Individual genes may behave as if they are 'selfish', but long, long ago they discovered that the most selfish thing they could do was to join a team and pull together. That's why replicators started banding together to build cells in the first place (see pp. 76-83). Then, thousands of millions of years later, those cells started working together to build bigger, more capable bodies. Eventually, some of those bodies began to look, think, feel and talk, like you do today.

So maybe Dawkins is right, and we really are all robots, built and guided by our genes (see pp. 84-5). But if so, we're the most unusual robots ever - robots who can choose to ignore some of the instructions programmed into their genes in order to genuinely understand and care for each other. Robots who realized long ago that we could only achieve great things by working together.

CHAPTER 7
Seeing the Light
HOW EVOLUTION INVENTED THE EYE

For the first four billion years of its existence, there wasn't a single eye on the whole of planet Earth. That didn't really bother its first inhabitants. They didn't need to be able to see. They were microbes that just kept on multiplying, creating vast swarms of living cells. Over aeons of time they spread through oceans, infiltrated rocks far below the seabed and began to ooze their way onto dry land.

The eye wasn't in any hurry to evolve either. It took thousands of millions of years for the first animals to start taking shape in the planet's seas; but even then, they couldn't see what was going on around them. It wasn't really a problem, though. Compared to today's frenetic pace of existence, life on a sightless planet was achingly slow.

THE BLIND PLANET – ANIMALS OF THE EDIACARAN PERIOD
(635–541 MILLION YEARS AGO)

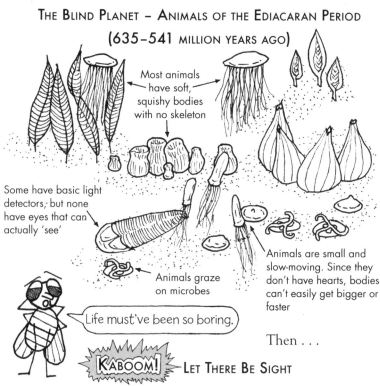

Around 540 million years ago, the first creature with eyes evolved. Called a trilobite, it looked like a giant mutant woodlouse, with two small compound eyes. After it arrived, the world got faster and more hectic. The *Cambrian period* of Earth's history had begun and the evolution of animal life went into overdrive:

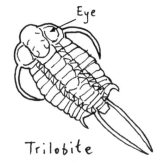

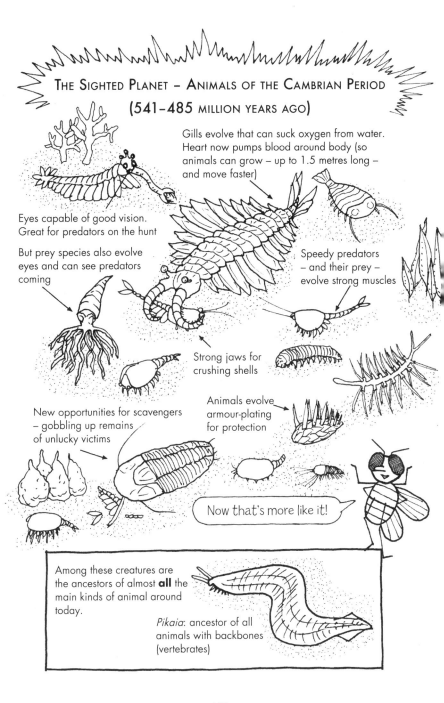

The start of the Cambrian was one of the most intense periods of evolutionary inventiveness ever – at least for animal life – which is why it's sometimes called the Cambrian Explosion. And, according to some biologists, that explosion was 'detonated' by the appearance of eyes. Once creatures could see – and be seen – they **all** had to adapt. Or die.

From this point in Earth's history onwards, the biggest factor driving evolutionary change had nothing to do with the non-living environment – the weather, the climate, sea level, etc. – and everything to do with the weird and wonderful **animals** that were evolving. As they got bigger, more varied and more capable, animals took on entirely new ways of living – as predators, prey, scavengers, parasites, etc. Even the single-celled organisms that had held sway before the animals arrived had to react, evolving new protections against microbe-munching predators, or turning themselves into parasites, diseases or scavengers. In short, the eye helped make life as a whole richer, more varied, more complex and more dangerous than ever before.

How Your Eyes Evolved

When it's in tip-top working order, it's hard not to be impressed by the human eye. Using a bunch of squidgy cells, evolution has crafted a genuine, super-high-definition 'camera'. It has a fully adjustable lens, it can detect millions of different colours, it can swivel in its socket and even wink at its friends.

In Darwin's day, some sceptics didn't believe evolution by natural selection could **possibly** explain how such a complicated structure as the human eye had taken shape.

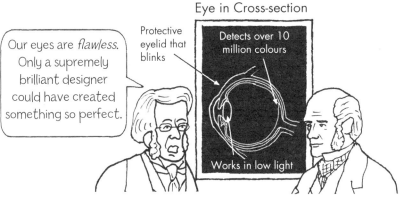

OK, we already know **you're** way better at detecting movement than we are, Fly (see pp. 8-9). But insects' compound eyes aren't perfect either.

A golden eagle can spot a rabbit three kilometres away. Giant ostracods live so deep under the sea that they never see sunlight, but their massive mirror-backed eyes can still operate brilliantly in the dark.

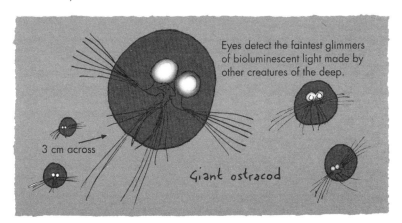

Because today's eyes come in all shapes and sizes, scientists can use them to understand how natural selection must have steered the eye's evolution.

> Reeeally? How's that even possible?

Evolution can only build complicated things like eyes gradually, step by step. And at every stage, even organisms whose eyes look 'part-formed' (compared to our eyes, anyway) must have found them useful. That's got to be true, because lots of living things are still using the same sorts of eye millions of years later. By looking at those creatures' eyes today, scientists have been able to work out the main stages our 'camera-like' eyes must have gone through as they evolved over the last billion years:

ONE BILLION YEARS TO BUILD AN EYE

Stage 1. The Simple Light Detector (first formed ~ one billion years ago) Single-celled photosynthesizing microbe called *chlamydomonas* – say *clammy-de-moan-us*.

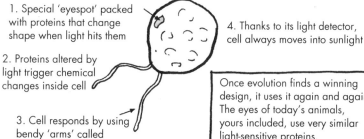

1. Special 'eyespot' packed with proteins that change shape when light hits them

2. Proteins altered by light trigger chemical changes inside cell

3. Cell responds by using bendy 'arms' called 'flagella' to swim towards light

4. Thanks to its light detector, cell always moves into sunlight

Once evolution finds a winning design, it uses it again and again. The eyes of today's animals, yours included, use very similar light-sensitive proteins.

Stage 2. The Cup-Shaped Eye (first formed ~600–550 million years ago) Many shellfish have very simple eyes:

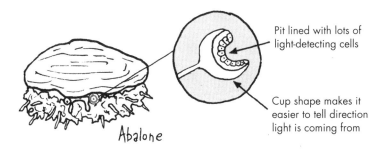

Stage 3. The Pinhole Eye (first formed ~541 million years ago) This is a nautilus:

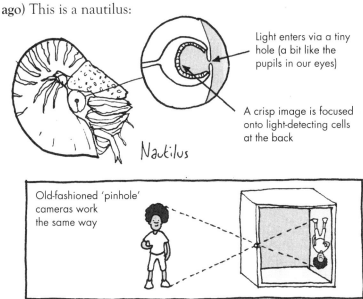

Trouble is, to get a good picture, the 'pupil' in these pinhole eyes has to be tiny, reducing the amount of light that can get in. So they only work well in bright conditions.

Stage 4. The Camera Eye (first formed ~540 million years ago) The trilobites evolved the eye's next major upgrade – the lens – during the Cambrian Explosion. Fly's eyes, and all today's insect eyes, still work in a similar way:

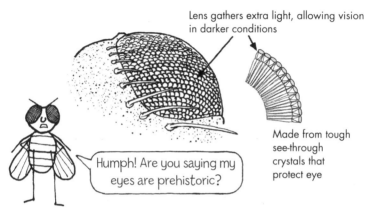

From Stage 4 onwards, it's been all about tweaking and rearranging the basic working parts to evolve all sorts of different kinds of eyeball, like those of the golden eagle, the giant ostracod and the human:

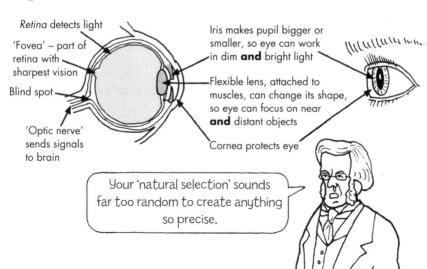

Actually, one thing you **can't** call natural selection is random. Sure, each new **mutation** crops up **at random**, and its **effect** is unpredictable – it might make cells in an eye grow a bit bigger or smaller or it might start making a totally new kind of protein, for example. But the way new genetic variations get tested is the **absolute opposite** of random. A variation that makes an eye work less well is more likely to be weeded out, whereas a variation that makes the eye more effective – e.g., if a new protein happened to work as a lens – has a greater chance of being reproduced. These variations can help an organism survive.

Generating mutations is a bit like blue-sky thinking.

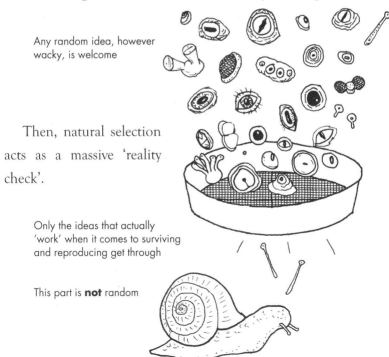

Any random idea, however wacky, is welcome

Then, natural selection acts as a massive 'reality check'.

Only the ideas that actually 'work' when it comes to surviving and reproducing get through

This part is **not** random

The adaptations that emerge from this process are often fantastically **creative** - natural selection comes up with surprising solutions to life's problems - but they are **not** random.

Evolution can't ever plan ahead, but let it run for enough time and the range of possible bodies and behaviours natural selection can create is virtually endless. The eye is just one example. Take a look at the world. It has conjured up spiders that weave webs, fungi that grow gigantic webs of mycorrhiza (see pp. 95-6) and human beings that built the worldwide web! As well as all the incredible adaptations that do exist, there's a whole universe of other possible designs that no living thing has evolved . . . yet.

Pah! Ever heard of fly swats, Fly? The thing is, when it comes to evolution, there's always room for improvement.

Why There's No Such Thing as Perfect

Imagine the perfect organism: it would be so amazingly matched to its surroundings that only the cruellest twist of fate - a volcanic eruption, an extreme storm or a meteorite impact – could cut its life short and stop it reproducing. Evolution will never create that creature, for all sorts of reasons. These are some of the big ones:

1. **The world keeps changing** The adaptations we see in the world around us today exist because they worked brilliantly in the past. They won't necessarily carry on working brilliantly for ever. For example, when the main threat small fish faced was bigger fish, sticking together in massive, swirling shoals made an individual fish much harder to catch. But today, fishing boats with enormous nets can scoop up the whole shoal in one go. Evolution can't predict how the world – and especially other organisms – will change; because of our greedy practices many marine species are at risk of *extinction* today.

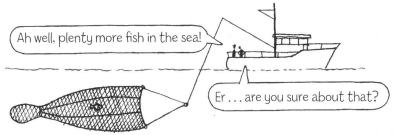

2. **History holds us back** In the 1950s, computers were so big they filled entire rooms. Imagine if the only way to make a **better** computer had always been to swap parts one at a time, at **random**. Now imagine the engineers had to make sure the computer worked even **better** than before after every single change. That's basically how living things evolve: by

tinkering with and trying to improve bodies that already exist. If computers had 'evolved' that way, you could expect your first smartphone to be delivered in, oh, a million years' time.

Evolution is brilliant at tinkering, but there's no avoiding the fact that it tends to move slowly.

Even today's humans can sometimes be held back by outdated body parts. Bumped the base of your spine, lately? The reason it's such agony is that you've got a little stub of a tail down there, called a 'coccyx'. It's really a 20-million-year-old relic from the time when your ancestors were monkeys with actual tails.

3. **Everything is a Compromise** Organisms constantly have to balance the risk of going hungry with the risk of being eaten or dying of disease. And time and energy spent dealing with those different threats means less time and energy spent reproducing. The individuals that pass the test of natural selection aren't absolutely perfect – they're the ones that find the most convenient **compromise solution**.

For example, cheetahs might be able to run even faster if they had slightly longer legs, supported by lighter leg bones. But those changes would make their legs more fragile. And a cheetah can't run at all – or stay alive – with a broken leg.

So the most successful cheetahs are those with legs that strike a balance between flat-out speed and robustness.

4. **Fads and Fashions** Parts of some animals' bodies look utterly impractical. Think of a peacock's tail:

Sigh! It took ages to grow, it's a nightmare to clean and predators can spot me a mile off!

Those extraordinary tails evolved because the distant ancestors of today's pea**hens** started finding males with flashier plumage more attractive. Through the generations, that trend really took off, since the males with bigger, brighter feathers gained a massive advantage: loads more chances to mate. This is a special kind of natural selection, called *sexual selection*. It's a reminder that trying to make the 'perfect organism' is more than simply keeping a creature healthy and well fed. Finding the adaptations needed to reproduce successfully is just as vital.

5. **Impossible Adaptations** Ever wondered why tortoises don't zoom around on wheels? It's because wheels need to roll freely around an axle. Any blood vessels, nerves or muscles that tried to cross the *axle* to keep the wheel alive would get hopelessly tangled. Some structures have never evolved because they simply **can't** evolve.

SURVIVORS

If you're using eyes to read these words you are living proof of evolution's awesome inventiveness. By sifting through **billions** of random mistakes that cropped up in **trillions** of individual DNA molecules over unimaginably huge expanses of time, natural selection fitted your head out with some of the most advanced **cameras** ever invented.

Nothing evolution creates is ever perfect, however, and the world does have a nasty habit of finding our weak spots. But every creature that's around today is still alive for one simple reason: they've found ways to overcome their imperfections and survive! The fact is, scientists reckon that over 99% of all the species that have ever existed are now extinct – their flaws, and the odd bit of bad luck, led to their ultimate downfall. But not us, Fly. We're the planet's great survivors!

CHAPTER 8
All Kinds of Everything
THE MIND-MELTING DIVERSITY OF LIVING THINGS

Living things come in **all shapes and sizes**.

From the tiniest virus.
A few millionths of a millimetre long

Zoomed in 10 million times

To the blue whale. 30 metres long. Largest animal that has ever existed

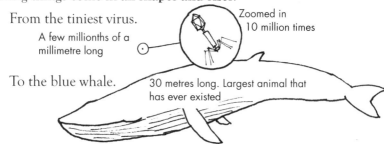

To the giant networks of squishy, branching tubes that make up a mycorrhizal fungus. Some cover more than nine square kilometres – making them the biggest organisms ever.

Forest

Mycorrhizal fungus

Do we actually know **how many** different creatures there are in the world?

Well, the honest answer is no. Creatures are pretty hard to count, for one thing:

- Some scarper when a scientist gets near.

- Some keep growing and changing shape, so identifying them is really tricky.

- Many live in hard-to-reach places – like the bottoms of putrid swamps or in boiling volcanic springs.

- Most living things are so small humans can't even see them.

Biologists have been trying to work out the total number of different life forms for hundreds of years, but even their very latest estimates vary wildly – from eight million to over a *million million* (i.e., one trillion)!

Back in the 1700s, a highly observant and extremely thorough Swedish scientist, called Carl Linnaeus, came up with a pretty good system for understanding life's diversity. Darwin hadn't even been born at this point, so Linnaeus didn't worry about evolution. In fact, he felt it was his duty to make sense of all God's creatures.

Deus creavit. Linnaeus disposuit.

That's Latin for '*God created, Linnaeus organized*'. He wasn't exactly modest.

Linnaeus started by collecting every plant and animal he

could lay his hands on and studying them obsessively. He grouped them into different species.

> Hang on a minute, what even is a 'species'?

That's a very good question. Even today biologists don't all agree on the answer. Put simply, a species is a particular 'kind' of living thing.

> I organized creatures into species by looking for characteristics that linked one creature to another creature but separated it from others.

Linnaeus gave each species a two-part Latin name.

Canis familiaris means 'family dog'.

Felis catus, means – er – 'cat cat'.

Dogs are more social

Cats can climb trees

Many dogs love to swim
Most cats don't

Dogs love to chase sticks
Cats are not interested in sticks

Cats are carnivores (eat meat)
Dogs are *omnivores* (eat anything)

Dogs wag their tails when happy
Cats purr when happy

Then Linnaeus came up with a clever way of grouping similar species into a series of gradually expanding 'boxes'. For example:

Categorizing all plants and animals like this was a mammoth task, but in 1735, Linnaeus began publishing all his work in a huge catalogue, called *Systema Naturae*, which means 'System of Nature'.

Soon people were sending Linnaeus specimens of living things from all over the world.

I was working day and night, hatching new species names, like a hen hatches her eggs!

By the time he released the 10th edition, in 1758–9, it included descriptions of over 13,000 species of plant and animal and Linnaeus was finally satisfied he'd seen and named most of the world's life forms.

He hadn't, though, had he?

Nope. Linnaeus did an amazing job, and, even today, most biologists still use a version of his 300-year-old naming and classification system.

But 13,000 species is tiny compared to today's best estimates of up to one trillion. And one reason Linnaeus massively undercounted was that he basically ignored all fungi, seaweeds and microscopic organisms.[*]

They're just insignificant little blobs of living matter!

Ha! Just you wait and see. . .

[*]He did know microbes existed. The Dutch scientist Antonie van Leeuwenhoek discovered them in 1673. See *Explodapedia: The Cell.*

Also, lumping creatures together based on their physical similarities and differences doesn't always work:

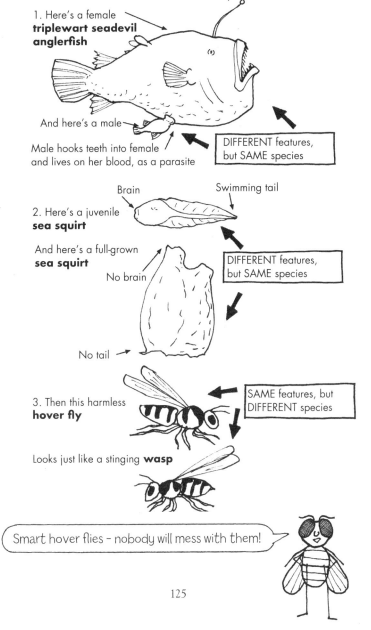

1. Here's a female **triplewart seadevil anglerfish**

And here's a male

Male hooks teeth into female and lives on her blood, as a parasite

DIFFERENT features, but SAME species

2. Here's a juvenile **sea squirt**

Brain — Swimming tail

And here's a full-grown **sea squirt**

No brain

No tail

DIFFERENT features, but SAME species

3. Then this harmless **hover fly**

Looks just like a stinging **wasp**

SAME features, but DIFFERENT species

Smart hover flies – nobody will mess with them!

Which is why today's biologists prefer to say that individual creatures only belong to the **same** species if they can breed together.

Great Danes and Chihuahuas **look** different but they **are** both kinds of dog and they **can** have puppies together – so they belong to the same species.

Actually, it's a bit more complicated than that. To qualify as a species, two parents must produce offspring that can have offspring of their own. For example:

Zebras and donkeys can mate and produce offspring. But their 'zedonk' babies can't reproduce. So zebras and donkeys belong to different species.

Focusing on cross-breeding helps biologists understand how one species can split into two.

Aha, like Darwin's finches did on page 45?

Exactly.

All that's needed is for a population to get divided – e.g., once the finches settled on the Galápagos Islands they could no longer mate with the finches on mainland South America, so they each went off along different evolutionary paths. The longer two populations stay apart, the more likely it is that they won't be able to cross-breed, or won't even try, if they meet again. That's when biologists say they've become two separate species. They call this process *speciation.*

But the cross-breeding test is totally useless for the enormous numbers of living things that *reproduce asexually.* We're talking bacteria, most other microbes, quite a lot of plants and fungi and even some animals (e.g., water fleas) that don't ever mate, because they can produce offspring without needing to mix their genes with the genes of another individual.

Scientists do their best to lump these organisms together according to their shared characteristics, just as Linnaeus did. It's a gargantuan task, but these days they have a powerful new tool to help them: *DNA sequencing.*

THE TREE OF LIFE

DNA sequencing shows that every species has its own distinctive pattern of genetic information, like the DNA 'barcodes' Morgan used to identify fruit fly genes (see p. 63), but even more detailed. These barcodes make it much easier to work out which species an organism belongs to. But it also lets biologists estimate **when** each species evolved and work out how **closely related** one species is to another.

How? Since new species can only form when a group of organisms splits off from an existing species – through speciation – the more **similar** two species' DNA is, the more **recently** they must have been part of the **same** species. Biologists draw these relationships as 'family trees'. Here's how that looks for some of the main kinds of vertebrate animal.

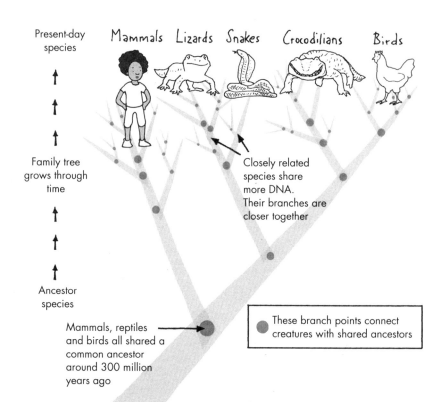

But Darwin floated the idea that **all** creatures are **related** – meaning every species is a twig on the **same** 'tree of life' (see p. 48). And now, 200 years later, DNA sequencing has proved his hunch to be absolutely right. It also shows us that the tree of life is bigger, lusher and more magnificent than even Darwin himself could have imagined.

Over the past 30 years, biologists have sequenced the DNA of hundreds of thousands of different species, from the very large to the infinitesimally small. The huge majority of Earth's species are minuscule microbes. Most haven't ever been seen – even through a microscope. Biologists only know about them because they've detected their DNA in samples taken from soil, rocks, seawater, hot springs, animal dung, etc.

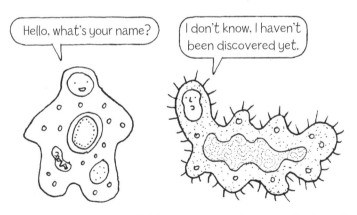

Even the tiniest microbe has a spot on the tree... So how do they all fit on it? Well, prepare to be amazed . . . here's how the tree looks for every species we've discovered so far:

1. **All life grows from ONE trunk** So a single living species can trace its origins back to the **same ancestor** species that scientists call the Last Universal Common Ancestor – or Luca, for short. Life must have started just **once**.*

2. **The tree has three main boughs** They are called the three 'domains' of life:
2a. **Bacteria** (*back-teary-a*) are small, simple single-celled life forms.
2b. **Archaea** (*are-kay-a*) look like bacteria, but inside they have some very different chemical reactions.
2c. **Eukaryotes** (*you-carry-oats*) All animals, plants and fungi are eukaryotes, including you. Eukaryote cells are usually more complicated than bacteria and archaea cells.

3. **All the species we can see (with the naked eye) are ONE part of ONE branch** Animals, plants, fungi and us humans are all newcomers to the tree, that's why we're balanced on this spindly branch.

4. **Parts of the tree are more like a tangled bush** Branches have even been known to fuse together. Unrelated microbes can swap genes with each other (called *horizontal gene transfer*).

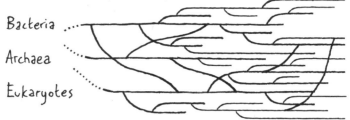

And, a handful of times, different living things have merged their whole lives. For example, around two billion years ago a bacteria cell ended up inside an archaea cell. The bacteria devoted its life to making energy – turning into structures called *mitochondria*, which work like miniature power stations inside cells – and together the bacteria and archaea cells became the first eukaryotes.

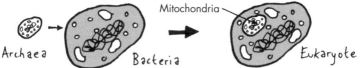

The tree keeps changing Every year scientists discover **thousands** of new life forms. Most are single-celled and tiny, but they all need a place on the tree. Some estimate that we've still only found 1% of all existing species!

*Actually, life may well have started more than once, but all the other attempts fizzled out long ago (or got gobbled up by Luca's descendants). More on this in *Explodapedia: The Cell*.

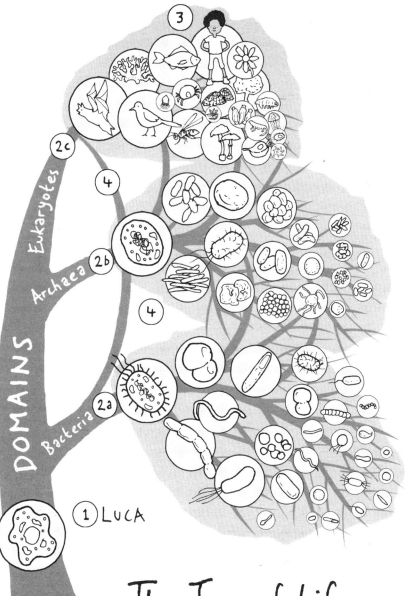

The Tree of Life

You've got to admit the tree of life is impressive.

Meh. Who cares about all those pointless little microbes?

Pointless? Microbes make the soil plants grow in! Without them, animal and plant waste simply wouldn't break down: we'd all be buried in it!

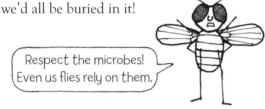

Respect the microbes! Even us flies rely on them.

Yup, no doubt about it. Microbes keep the whole world going.

But why the heck are there are **SO MANY** species?

Well, the fact is, life is **really** challenging – species go extinct all the time. So, whenever a new opportunity for eking out a living appears, organisms will always try to snatch it – like they did after the Cambrian Explosion on pages 106-8. Basically, the evolution of one new species almost always creates opportunities for more new species. Just take a look at your own body to see who jumped on board after humans evolved. . .

You Are an Ecosystem

Every surface of your body – inside and out – has billions of resident microbes, and some slightly larger animal inhabitants

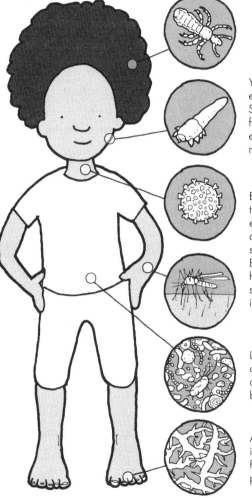

We humans have our very own, personalized lice species! Head lice **only** drink **human** blood

Your skin is crawling with eight-legged skin mites. Some hide inside hair follicles on your face and eat the oily stuff your skin makes to stop it drying out

Even microbes that trigger diseases – e.g., tonsilitis, malaria and COVID 19 – can't survive without us. Because **we** exist, **they** have evolved ways to survive and reproduce inside our bodies

Large intestine: contains up to 1,000 different species of bacteria

Athlete's foot – itchy infection caused by fungus that feeds on proteins in your skin

The microbes that live on you form part of your body called your 'microbiome'. A healthy microbiome stops you getting hungry, malnourished or ill.

And, it sounds gross, but if *decomposers* and *detritivores* didn't break down and **recycle** the chemical parts found in poo and dead bodies, all that goodness would be lost to the world for ever. Without decay, life can't keep growing.

So, you are much more than just a human being; 'your' body is an entire *ecosystem*. Each of its non-human members have evolved specifically to thrive within a particular part of your ecosystem, called a *niche*. Some help you, some can harm you, others are just along for the ride.

And that's just humans! The survival of every living species is deeply bound up with the lives of all kinds of **other** species – they all create opportunities for new life:

- Every plant can feed a *herbivore*.
- Every herbivore can feed a carnivore.
- Every animal and every plant is home for the creatures of its microbiome.

- Every living body can fall victim to a parasite or disease.
- Every dead body, and every scrap of bodily waste, can feed a scavenger or a decomposer.

Organisms crop up in every imaginable habitat in every corner of the planet – the deepest seas, the coldest ice caps, the hottest deserts, the highest clouds – so there's an eye-wateringly massive number of niches available for evolution to fill. And, therefore, an equally massive number of species.

Even more amazing is the fact that all this endless diversity sprouted from the **same tree**.

Life is one enormous family.

Exactly. You don't just need all the species that make up your microbiome, you're related to every single one of them, including Fly – and her microbiome.

Yep. We're all connected, through the branches of the tree of life, to every other species, living and extinct.

And that means, dear reader, you're also related, via a massive chain of ancestors, to the planet's very first living things. That chain starts with your parents, grandparents and great grandparents and ends up, countless millions of 'greats' earlier, with Luca. Some of your ancestors were human; most definitely were not. But they all lived long enough to reproduce successfully. As we're about to discover, all of their 'successes', through round after round of natural selection, have combined to shape the body you live in, and the life you lead, right now.

CHAPTER 9
You're History, Sunshine
LIFE BUILDS ON WHAT CAME BEFORE

The title of this chapter isn't a threat, by the way. It's literally true – it took four billion years for the tree of life to grow to its current shape. That means it's also taken four billion years to build the human body and all other life forms that still exist today. The fact is, every single part of our bodies evolved **before** our species even existed. That's how evolution works: it can only modify what's already there. Usually, it doesn't even bother to dismantle any outdated structures. Instead, like over-eager DIY enthusiasts, evolving life forms just keep on redecorating, renovating, repairing and remodelling their homes.

So, like it or not, you're a living, breathing, walking, talking, thinking jumble of patched-together 'home improvements' (though quite a high-achieving one!). Throughout evolution, your ancestors developed new features – basically adding new 'selves' to the thing you call 'yourself'. The following are the key stages of the never-ending construction project otherwise known as 'the human':

Stage 1. The Self-reproducing 'Caravan': Your Ancient Microbe Self (~4,000–3,500 million years ago)

The planet's very first cells were like the most self-contained 'mobile homes' ever. They had everything they needed to suck energy and chemical raw materials out of their environment, and put them to work **reproducing** themselves. And, every time they reproduced, they had to copy all their DNA. The main *enzymes* they used for DNA copying worked brilliantly. That's part of the reason they're still used – give or take a few design tweaks – by **all** of today's living things, from bacteria to barnacles to blue whales to blueberry bushes.

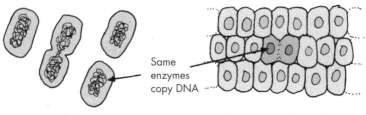

Bacteria cells dividing   Same enzymes copy DNA   Human skin cells dividing

Stage 2. New 'Fixtures and Fittings': Your Eukaryote Self (~2,000 million years ago)

The first major upgrades happened when cells started installing a range of fancy new internal 'appliances' – biology's own versions of ovens, blenders, vacuum cleaners, food stores, etc. These structures are called *organelles*. The most important organelles were the 'power generators' or mitochondria. Mitochondria helped the eukaryote cell take shape (see p. 130). The first eukaryote cells are the ancestors of all of today's animals, fungi and plants – which explains why they **all** still use the **same** kind of mitochondria today.

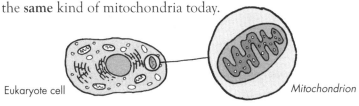

Eukaryote cell · Mitochondrion

Stage 3. The 'Shanty Town': Your Sponge-Like Self (~700–600 million years ago)

The first multicellular 'buildings' probably looked a bit like shabby versions of today's sea sponges:

1. Water sucked through spongey body
2. Filters out microbes and bits of detritus as food
3. Water ejected

Even so, the 'cements' they used to connect all the different cell 'rooms' together worked brilliantly – proteins made by the descendants of the same genes hold together the cells that make up your body today.

Protein 'cements' stick cells together

Stage 4. 'Indoor Plumbing': Your Worm Self (~580 million years ago)

Yup, we humans are actually modified worms.

But that's true for you too, Fly. Humans, flies and 99% of **all** today's animals are descendants of a worm-like creature called an 'urbilaterian'. It was one of the first animals to install a proper internal plumbing system, by developing a gut and becoming 'tube-shaped'.

Its shape automatically gave urbilatarian:

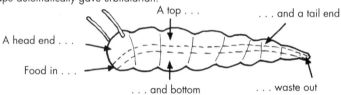

Urbilatarian could move, too – thanks to newly evolved muscles and nerves – so its practical way of life quickly caught on. The only animals alive today that haven't developed from that basic worm shape are comb jellies, sponges, corals and a handful of other critters.

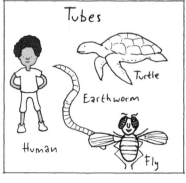

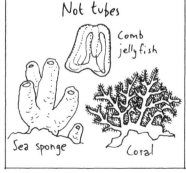

Stage 5. 'Mission Control': Your Baby Sea Squirt Self (~535 million years ago)

Once animals were on the move, fitted with eyes (see pp. 106–8), hunting, and being hunted, a 'mission control centre', aka a brain, became the next 'must-have' body part. One of the first creatures to evolve a **brain** was the ancestor you share with today's sea squirts (see p. 125). You've got a lot in common with a juvenile sea squirt (or *larva*), even if it does look like a tadpole. As well as a brain, sea squirt larvae have a bundle of nerves running through their bodies, supported by a rod of toughened tissue called a 'notochord'. Your *embryo* had the same structures – they turned into your spine and spinal cord. They support your body, co-ordinate your movements and mark you out as a vertebrate – together with all fish, reptiles, birds, mammals and amphibians.

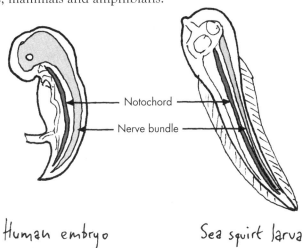

Human embryo   Sea squirt larva

Stage 6. The 'Air Conditioning System': Your Lungfish Self (~415 million years ago)

Ever wondered why you get hiccups? Some scientists think it's an evolutionary 'memory' from the time when our ancestors were a kind of fish that had 'water-breathing' gills **and** 'air-breathing' lungs. There was much less oxygen in the atmosphere and the seas back then. Having lungs meant these fishy relatives could come up for gulps of air whenever they needed extra oxygen. These two breathing systems were controlled by an automatic reflex that switched from one to the other. When your ancestors left the seas for good, their gills shrank but the reflex didn't completely disappear: that's what causes your hiccups.

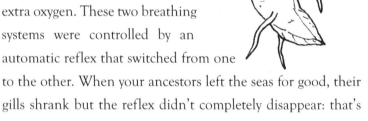

Stage 7. Building on Old Foundations: Your Amphibian Self (~350 million years ago)

Why is practically everyone born with **five** toes and **five** fingers?

It's actually an accident of history: we evolved from an amphibious ancestor that just so happened to crawl around on **four** legs that each ended in five toes (what biologists call a *pentadactyl tetrapod* – which just means a 'five-fingered, four-legged animal').

The bones inside a bird's wing, a cheetah's paw, a mole's hand, a whale's flipper, a gecko's foot and a bat's wing are all variations on the **same** five-digit theme. Why? Because they all evolved from the **same pentadactyl** ancestors.

Stage 8. More Power, More Heat: Your Ancient Reptile Self (~250 million years ago)

The heart that beats away inside your chest has four different chambers. It's a brilliant design, mainly because it stops blood that's loaded with life-sustaining oxygen from mixing with blood that's low on oxygen. You inherited this kind of heart from reptile ancestors that you share with all other mammals, crocodiles and dinosaurs (including the ones that evolved into birds). Without the four-chambered heart, biologists think dinosaurs could never have grown so big . . .

As long as three school buses and as heavy as nine!

. . . and birds could never have taken flight.

Come on. I can do this!

Stage 9. The 'Security Sensors': Your Tree Shrew Self (~ 185 million years ago)

When the dinosaurs ruled the roost, your ancestors were timid little mammals that only dared come out at night. They hunted insects in the dark, so, for security, they needed a brilliant sense of smell. Scientists know this because all of today's mammal species, including humans, contain around 1,000 different genes for making proteins called *olfactory receptors*. Each one is tailor-made for detecting a different chemical smell.

Keen sense of smell helps with finding food

But, in humans, around 600 of our 1,000 olfactory receptor genes have picked up so many mutations they no longer work. That's because, more recently, our ancestors (e.g., see Stage 10) started to rely on their eyes more than their noses.

> So, if you don't use it you lose it!

Stage 10. The 'Tree House': Your Monkey Self (~50 million years ago)

Thumbs up if you think hands are cool! Some scientists have argued that nimble fingers and powerful gripping thumbs were one of the main adaptations that helped our Stone Age ancestors to start making tools. But almost every other species of monkey and ape has fingers **and** thumbs too. So the hand must have evolved earlier to allow your primate ancestors to swing through the trees.

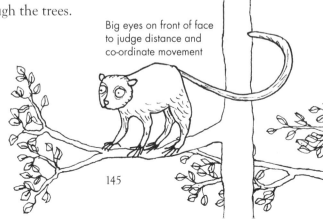

Big eyes on front of face to judge distance and co-ordinate movement

Stage 11. Standing Tall: Your Hominin Self (~4.4 million years ago)

Gradually, our primate ancestors started spending less time in the trees and more time roaming the open grasslands of Africa. Some began to look more recognizably 'human'. But, like most big steps in evolution, humans didn't start standing tall overnight: the oldest known species of upright *hominin*, called *Ardipithecus ramidus*, still spent quite a bit of time on all fours.

Well, birds turned their two freed-up limbs into wings. And when our human ancestors stood up, they didn't just get a better view, they found they could use their hands for all kinds of useful jobs – like hurling spears. And swatting uppity flies.

Stage 12. The Finishing Touches: Your Human Self (~300,000 years ago)

Most of the building work was done by the time *Homo sapiens* evolved. But we weren't the only human beings around and compared to our 'cousin' species, Homo neanderthalensis (or 'Neanderthals'), our construction was a little flimsy.

Our brains had been growing ever since 'Stage 5', but **theirs** had too. In fact, their brains were bigger than ours. Recent studies of Neanderthal DNA and fossils suggest that, like us, they could probably use language to communicate.

Homo sapiens shared the world with Neanderthals and other (now-extinct) human species for over 250 thousand years. After the next stage, our species started taking over.

Stage 13. Installing the 'Internet': Your Co-operative Human Self (~80,000–50,000 years ago)

The most recent major upgrades to the human being may have been totally invisible, but they made an enormous difference. Some scientists think that a small number of genetic mutations altered the wiring of the Homo sapiens brain in subtle, but life-changing, ways. If this idea is right, it means our ancestors started using more sophisticated language, and their imaginations quite suddenly expanded.* They got better at predicting the future and hatched increasingly elaborate plans for outwitting other humans and hunting bigger, wilier prey. The stories they swapped around camp fires turned into myths and legends that gave each group of humans a **shared identity**. Instead of only co-operating with close relatives (see kin selection, p. 93), people were working with their entire tribe and elders were sharing with younger generations everything they'd learned in a lifetime.

The number of ideas in the world – about how to cook, catch, carve, chat, care, cure, clean and pretty much everything else – grew and grew. These ideas gradually became part of an enormous shared pool of knowledge and 'know-how'. Scientists call this a ***collective intelligence,*** because it belongs to whole groups of co-operating *Homo sapiens*.

Other human species seem to have died out 30–15,000 years ago. Maybe they didn't learn to work together so well?

With their upgraded brains and new skills, *Homo sapiens* found they were able to adapt to pretty much everything life threw at them. They became the planet's most feared predators and spread out across the whole globe, aiming to tame and control the rest of the natural world as they went.

Pah! You never tamed us!

*Other scientists argue that our old brains just gradually learned new tricks.

Since then, natural selection has tweaked the *Homo sapiens* genome here and there – for example, since people started farming, around 10-6,000 years ago, the human digestive system has evolved so that today most of us can eat ice cream and pizza without getting indigestion. Apart from minor adaptations like these, 'the human' hasn't been through any major refurbishments since. In fact, if you could transport a Stone Age child to our times, wash them, cut their hair and dress them in modern clothes, they'd soon fit right in . . . well almost . . .

> Won't we eventually evolve more cool stuff like wings and telepathic powers?

Hmm... probably not. Genes pick up a few mutations with every new generation, so we **are** still evolving. Humans from the very distant future might eventually look quite different from us. But they almost certainly won't have wings. There's just too much that would have to change for wings to work on humans: our bones are too heavy, our hearts too weak, our muscles too puny and our hands too useful. And, crucially, there'd need to be a really good evolutionary reason to start altering it all: children born with even the tiny beginnings of wing-like arms would need those stubs to give them some sort of massive advantage when it came to surviving and reproducing.

Besides, even if those changes could start happening, gene-based evolution is painfully slow...

> Yeah, you lot take decades to make a new generation!

... Ever since Stage 13, it's not so much our bodies that have been evolving as our **ideas**. This has been happening for thousands of years already – and ideas can change far faster than genomes – but it's speeding up in the 21st century. From now on, it's what we do with all our ideas that will shape our lives the most.

Thanks to our ever-expanding collective intelligence, we've come up with technologies that would make our ancestors from 200 years ago – let alone 200,000 years ago – believe we are **actual magicians**. Just stepping into a really hot shower would have been the stuff of dreams for most people only a few generations ago. What if they could see how we:

• Soar through the heavens, in a plane, helicopter, hot air balloon or rocket?

• Summon almost **anyone** and **any idea** into our own living rooms at any time, via video calls and internet searches?

• Cure and prevent diseases that once spelled certain death, thanks to *antibiotics* and *vaccines*?

• Have developed machines that can write poetry and solve seemingly impossible science problems through *artificial intelligence*?

• Can even alter or replace any gene in a baby's genome, potentially creating *genetically enhanced* humans through *gene editing*?[*]

Scientists gather more knowledge and innovations get more powerful every year. And the more ideas we have, the faster they change our world. The question is, can we use our 'magical powers' to build a healthier, safer and more enjoyable life for **everyone**?

[*]More on this in *Explodapedia: The Gene*.

Is This the End, or the Beginning?

This blue-green planet of ours is so completely covered with living things, we sometimes forget how incredible they all are. And yet, scientists have never once detected the tiniest flicker of life **anywhere else** in the universe. Most of space really does seem to be an endless, lifeless nothingness.*

But if we do one day discover alien life forms – or they discover us – it's almost certain that, just like all life on Earth, they will:

1. Be based on chemical reactions.
2. Have evolved by natural selection.

So that's all there is to life? Just chemical reactions and evolution...

---

*Space is also mind-meltingly enormous, however. Scientists estimate that there are billions of 'Earth-like' planets – which **could** support Earth-like life forms – elsewhere in the universe.

What d'you mean 'just'?! It's amazing! It's everything! Look at what chemical reactions and evolution achieved: together, they took a bunch of random atoms and molecules and wove them into the awesomely complicated, growing, reproducing, persevering, jaw-droppingly beautiful collections of chemical reactions that we call **living things**.

And, after many millions of years of evolution, natural selection turned some bundles of linked-up chemical reactions into brains. Some of those brains eventually got smart enough to figure out how evolution works – and understand how they came to exist in the first place.

In other words, natural selection, acting on chemical reactions, ended up making extraordinary people like **YOU**.

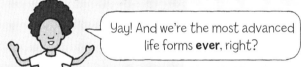

Yay! And we're the most advanced life forms **ever**, right?

We really can't say that. All of today's species are just as 'highly evolved' – or they wouldn't be alive! Lots of them can do extremely 'advanced' things that we can only dream of, such as:

• Turning sunlight, air and water into fruit.

So ... I'm tasting sunshine and eating air?

- Navigating over thousands of kilometres, without a map or compass.

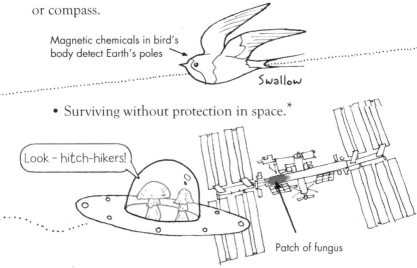

- Surviving without protection in space.*

Besides, it's **far too early** to tell whether we're going to be one of evolution's great success stories. In the grand scheme of things, humans have only just arrived. If life's history was a feature-length movie, we'd only appear in the very last frame of the very last scene.

And the plot of that movie could easily have taken all sorts of different turns. For example, if the giant meteorite that exterminated most of the dinosaurs had touched down just a few seconds earlier than it did, it would have plunged deep into the ocean. The explosion would have been **much smaller** and our mammal ancestors might never have got their chance to replace the ruling giant reptiles. Instead of you, there could

*Living fungus, originally from Earth, really has been seen to survive as long as a year on the **outside** of the International Space Station.

have been a super-intelligent dinosaur descendant sitting here reading a book about evolution.

Yes, we've figured out how to do some impressive stuff in the brief scene we've been part of. We can farm, fight off illnesses, travel the world by land, air and sea, stay connected via the internet and keep our cities stocked with fresh water and energy.

Tsk. You behave as if you **own** the place.

Er. You have a point there, Fly. In truth, a lot of what we've done to make **our** lives easier has just caused the rest of the world a whole load of headaches. Here are just a few of the big ones:

• We've used *fossil fuels* so much it's triggered the climate crisis.

• We're eating our way through most of the fish in the sea.

• We're polluting every natural ecosystem with plastic and other rubbish.

It's got to the point where we're altering the entire planet so much that the rules of evolution are changing for pretty much all other life forms.

But other organisms can adapt, can't they? That's what's so cool about evolution.

Well, some of them are adapting. In the UK, for example, birds like great tits are laying their eggs three weeks earlier, because the warming climate means the caterpillars they feed on are hatching earlier than they used to. But evolution usually moves slowly, remember? Many species simply can't keep up with the human hunger for 'more'. Biologists say we're in the middle of a *mass extinction* **right now**, one that wouldn't be happening if we hadn't evolved. They estimate that species are going extinct 100 to 1,000 times faster than they were before humans existed.

Microbes, fungi, plants and animals are all vanishing before we can even discover them!

Life on Earth isn't just there to look pretty – it's literally what keeps us alive. Because of our shared evolution, all life is connected – every species depends on a whole web of **other creatures**. Cut too many strands in that web and the whole thing will eventually fall apart. The fact is we **need** the bacteria, fungi, beetles and earthworms that build the soils. We **need** the insects that pollinate our crops. And, above all, we **need** the plants that produce most of our food, make some of the oxygen we breathe, slow down climate change (by soaking up carbon dioxide), hold back floods and provide nearly half of all our medicines. When we harm nature, we're actually harming ourselves.

Suddenly I'm not feeling so 'advanced'...

Well there's one thing about us that definitely is advanced: our brains. We're the first creatures that have evolved to be fully **aware** of what we're doing to the world.

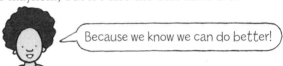

What about me?

You didn't evolve, Fly. You were invented by the author. Besides, you can't use science to understand the consequences of your actions. We can. It's depressing to realize that we're the cause of all this mayhem, but it's also the best news ever.

Because we know we can do better!

Precisely. No other creature has evolved the same ability to **decide** to change its habits. Now we need to mend our ways to stop the extinctions and start repairing the damage we've done to our planet's ecosystems.

I didn't name our species *Homo sapiens* for nothing!

Of course not. Our Latin name does indeed mean 'wise human'.

Wise? You lot? You've got to be kidding...

We still have time to prove you wrong, Fly. There are already plenty of brilliant planet-saving ideas around. As they leap from brain to brain, reproducing and mutating, they **evolve**, getting more powerful as they go:

Modern wind turbine: 300 metres tall. 10,000 times more powerful than a traditional windmill. Its clean electricity replaces fossil fuels

Traditional windmill: 20 metres tall. Grinds flour

And it's not just technology that is evolving. Each year more countries understand why it's in their own best interests to ban more pollutants and expand their national parks and support efforts to rewild* damaged landscapes. We can all do our bit to help bright ideas like these grow and spread. For example,

*Find out more in *Explodapedia: Rewild.*

we can try to buy the most *sustainable* food and clothing, join environmental campaigns, invite more wildlife into our gardens . . . and just talk to the people around us about the grave challenges the natural world faces – and the solutions that can fix them.

There's still a **long way** to go, of course. But as with evolution, small changes add up. If every human can be inspired to do the 'wise' thing, together we really can start breathing fresh life back into our world.

We sneaked in at the very end of *The Movie of Life: Part One*, but our role in the sequel could be non-existent, or it **could** be truly epic. If we play our part right now, evolution will see us sharing the screen with a dazzling array of creatures. Some will be familiar, others very unfamiliar, but they'll all be stars of the most spectacular show in the known universe.

I'm ready for my close-up!

TIMELINE OF EARTH AND THE EVOLUTION OF ALL LIVING THINGS

Living creatures on this timeline are shown at the estimated time they first appeared on Earth.

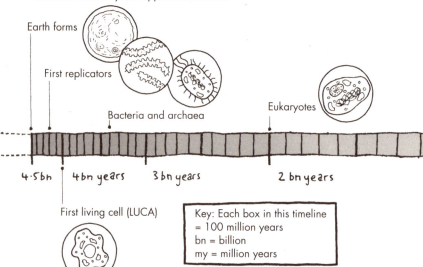

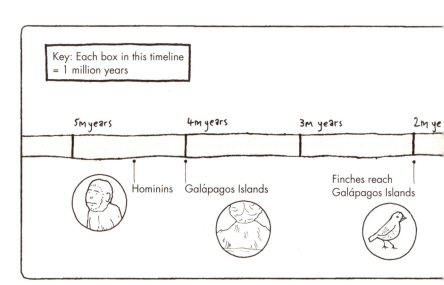

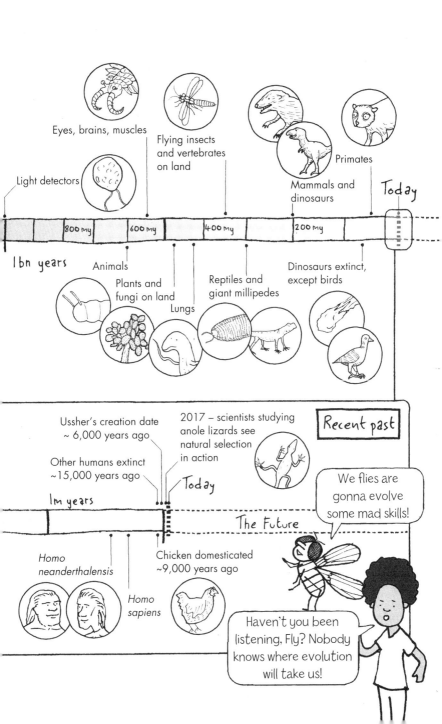

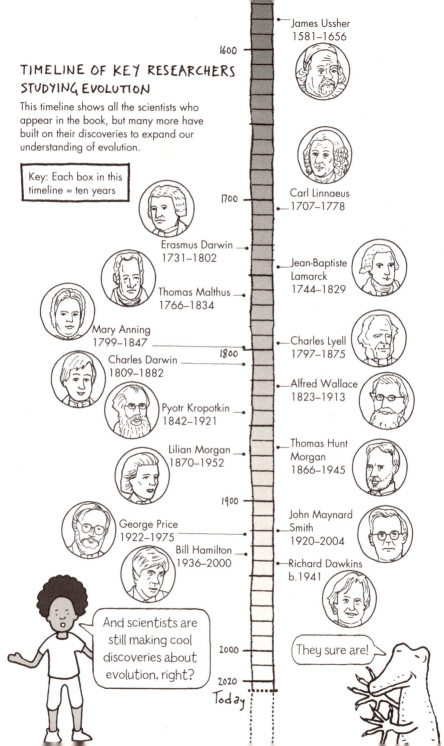

Glossary

Words italicized in this glossary have their own entries.

adaptation a *characteristic* that has developed over time through *natural selection* to help an *organism* survive and reproduce in its *environment*
algae varied group of *organisms* that *photosynthesize*, but are not plants
ancestor a *species* or individual from whom a living thing is directly descended
antibiotic medicine used to treat infections caused by *bacteria*
archaea tiny single-celled *organisms*. One of the main kinds of *microbe*
Ardipithecus ramidus one of the first *species* of *hominin* who could walk on two legs. Lived in East Africa around 4.4 million years ago
artificial intelligence computer programs designed to solve problems, often thinking and learning in much the same way a human brain thinks and learns
artificial selection when humans identify *organisms* with specific *characteristics* and deliberately ensure those characteristics are passed down to future generations
axle a rod that passes through the centre of a wheel or wheels
bacteria tiny single-celled *organisms*. One of the main kinds of *microbe*
BCE before the *Common Era*
biofilm a thin but strong layer of *microbes*, joined together by sticky substances made by the *cells* themselves
Cambrian period approximately 541 to 485 million years ago, when lots of different kinds of animal first evolved
carnivore an animal that eats other animals
cell the smallest thing that can definitely be called 'alive'. Cells live on their own as single cells, or together as parts of larger bodies
cell division when single *cells* make more cells by copying their *genes*

and then splitting into two

characteristic a feature that belongs to a certain individual or group

chemical bond a powerful force that holds atoms and/or *molecules* together

chemical reaction when one or more chemical substances are converted into different chemical substances

chlamydomonas a type of green *algae*, commonly found in fresh water

chromosomes long *DNA molecules*, with *proteins* attached, that contain a *cell's genes*

climate crisis disruptive changes in the global climate due to the warming of Earth's surface. Caused mainly by human activities that lead to the build-up of 'greenhouse gases' in the atmosphere

collective intelligence knowledge gained and shared by groups of individuals

Common Era (CE) the time period from year 1 – in the world's most widely used calendar – up to the present

cystic fibrosis a life-threatening, inherited health condition involving the build-up of mucus in the lungs, digestive tract and other areas of the body

decomposer/detritivore an *organism* that breaks down and consumes dead animal, plant or *microbe* matter

detritus waste or debris

dinosaur pre-historic reptiles that first evolved around 243 million years ago

DNA (deoxyribonucleic acid) long, string-like *molecules* that carry information and form a *cell's genes*

DNA sequencing the process of determining the order of the four *nucleotides* in *DNA*

ecosystem a community of *organisms* that interact with one another, and with the *environment* they live in

embryo a living thing going through its earliest stages of development

environment the surroundings or conditions a living thing exists in, including other living things it interacts with

enzyme a substance in a *cell* that can make, break, change or join together different kinds of *molecule*

eukaryote a living thing whose *chromosomes* are contained inside an *organelle* called a nucleus. Animals, plants and *fungi* are all eukaryotes

evolution the way the inherited *characteristics* of living things change over multiple generations

exoskeleton a skeleton on the outside of a body

extinct/extinction when a *species* no longer has any living members in existence

fertilize when two *cells* fuse together to make a new *embryo*

food chain a sequence showing how an array of different *organisms* get their food by eating each other

fossil/fossilized the preserved remains or traces of ancient *organisms* that lived long ago

fossil fuels ancient remains of plants and animals that people use as sources of energy – e.g., coal, oil and natural gas

fungus/fungi mushrooms, yeasts, toadstools, mildews, moulds and infections like 'athlete's foot'. They can be single *cells* or collections of cells, and feed on decaying material or other living things

gene/genetic each gene contains a specific instruction for how to build a particular part of a *cell* or body. Genes are made from DNA and passed down from one generation of a living thing to the next

gene editing using technology to make precise changes to the DNA of *cells* or living things

gene-centred view the theory that it is *genes*, not whole *organisms*, that benefit from *evolution* by *natural selection*, since it is genes that are passed on to the next generation

genetic code the way the instruction *cells* used to make RNA and *protein molecules* are stored inside DNA genes

genetically enhanced when scientists modify a living thing's *genes* in order to give it particular *characteristics*

genome the complete set of *genetic* instructions in an *organism*

geologist a scientist who studies the Earth and what it's made of

herbivore an *organism* that feeds on plants alone

hominin today's humans and all their *ancestors*, going back to the time when humans started evolving separately from the other apes

Homo neanderthalensis a *species* of early human who lived in parts of Asia and Europe approximately 300,000 to 30,000 years ago

Homo sapiens the *species* you belong to. Modern humans

horizontal gene transfer when *genes* are passed between different *organisms* that are not parent and offspring

hydrothermal vent a crack or 'fissure' in the seabed through which hot water and gases escape, mixing with seawater

inherit/inheritance receive a *genetic characteristic* from a parent or *ancestor*

kin selection a kind of *natural selection* that favours *characteristics* that help an *organism's* relatives to survive and *reproduce*, even if the organism itself may then be less able to survive and reproduce

larva a young animal that must go through significant physical change before becoming an adult – e.g. the tadpole, which eventually becomes a frog

malaria a disease caused by *parasites*. The parasites are transmitted to humans by infected mosquitoes

mass extinction when a large proportion of Earth's living *species* go *extinct* during the same period of time

mega-tsunami a massive, powerful wave, usually created by a large earthquake/volcanic eruption under the sea

membrane a thin layer made of fat-like 'lipid' *molecules* that surrounds a *cell*

microbe a living thing that is too small to be seen without a microscope

mitochondrion (plural **mitochondria**) a structure inside living *cells* where *chemical reactions* take place that are needed to produce crucial energy-carrying *molecules*

molecule two or more atoms joined together by *chemical bonds*

multicellular *organisms* made of lots of *cells*

mutation a change in a *gene* or *chromosome's* DNA structure, which might be passed down through generations

mutualism a relationship between two different *organisms* that benefits both of them

mycorrhiza *fungi* that surround a plant's roots and exchange nutrients with those roots

natural selection a process that drives *evolution*. Individuals born with inherited *characteristics* that suit their surroundings are more likely to survive and *reproduce*. Over the generations, the *genes* responsible for the beneficial *characteristics* become more common

neutral mutation a change in a *DNA* sequence that neither benefits nor harms a living thing's ability to survive and *reproduce*

niche a specific role that a living *species* has evolved to play within its *ecosystem*

nucleotide the basic building blocks of *DNA*

olfactory receptor a part of a *cell* that detects a specific 'smell *molecule*' and activates nerve impulses that send information about smells to the brain

omnivore animals that eat a variety of other animals, plants and *microbes*

organelle a part of a *cell* with a particular function – e.g., the *mitochondria* produce energy for a cell

organism a living thing

palaeontologist a scientist who learns about the history of life by studying *fossils*

parasite an *organism* that lives in or on another organism, getting benefits from its host without giving anything back

pentadactyl tetrapod five-fingered, four-legged animal

phosphorus a chemical element that all living things need in order to function and grow

photosynthesis/photosynthesize the process through which *cells* of a plant or *algae* use energy from sunlight to convert water and carbon dioxide into energy-containing sugar *molecules*

plankton small *organisms* that drift/float in water

plesiosaur reptiles that lived in the oceans around 215 to 66 million years ago

primate a group of mammals that includes humans, monkeys and apes

protein a large *molecule* that is essential for all living things. Proteins have many functions in *cells* – e.g., building structures and controlling *chemical reactions*

pterosaur a flying reptile that existed at the same time as the *dinosaurs*

pupa an insect in the stage of development between being a *larva* and an adult

reflex an automatic response to something – eg. quickly moving your hand away when it touches something hot

reproduce/reproduction to produce new copies of a living *cell* by *cell division*; or to make a new generation of living things

retina the *cells* at the back of your eye that detect light and send information to your brain about what you're seeing

ribonucleic acid (RNA) a chemical similar to *DNA*. One of its main jobs is delivering instructions from *genes* to the rest of the *cell*

sex cells *cells* needed for *sexual reproduction* – e.g., egg cells and sperm cells in animals

sexual reproduction when a male and a female *reproduce* by combining their *sex cells* to make a new *organism* which inherits *characteristics* from both parents

sexual selection *natural selection* caused by competition between living things for sexual partners

Siberia a huge region in the north of Russia, where it is often incredibly cold

sickle-cell disease an illness affecting red blood *cells*, which can cause pain, infections and swelling of hands and feet

social insects *species* of insect where individuals must co-operate in order to survive

speciation when new *species* are formed through *evolution*

species a specific kind of *organism*. The members of a species have similar *characteristics* and shared relatives

sustainable able to last for a long time, and/or meeting our own needs today, without affecting the ability of future generations to meet their own needs

termite *social insects* that often eat wood

theology the study of religion

vaccine a substance that can be put into our bodies to give us long-lasting protection against a disease

variation differences between individuals of the same *species*

virus a minuscule living particle that can only *reproduce* inside the *cells* of a different living thing. Some can cause diseases

INDEX

A

adaptations 24, 29, 33, 44, 46, 47, 53, 54, 73, 108, 114–15, 118, 145, 149, 155–6
algae 97
amphibians 142–3
Anning, Mary 34–5, 162
ants 89–90, 92–3, 98, 100, 102
archaea 130, 160
artificial selection 23–4, 43
asexual reproduction 127

B

bacteria 51, 61, 66, 67, 69, 98, 127, 130, 133, 138, 156, 160
Beagle, HMS 30, 31, 32, 39
beaks 20, 29, 39, 41, 46, 47
birds 19–21, 24–5, 29, 38–9, 40–1, 45–7
Boveri, Theodor 61, 63
brain 8, 13, 14, 21, 29, 73, 102–3, 141, 147–8, 153, 157, 161

C

Cambrian period/Cambrian Explosion 106–8, 112, 132
cell division 67, 68
cell membranes 81
cells 61, 67–8, 70–1, 82, 104
characteristics 20, 26, 27, 28, 44, 53, 122
chemical reactions 74–5, 77, 152–3
chickens 19, 22–4
chlamydomonas 110
chromosomes 61–3, 65, 67
climate crisis 26, 155–6
co-operation 88–9, 92–8, 100, 102, 103, 104, 148
collective intelligence 148, 151

colonies, ant 89–93, 100
common ancestor 47, 48, 107, 128–9, 130–1, 136, 139–146
competition 27, 28, 47, 102, 103
compound eyes 8, 106, 109
compromise solutions 116–17
coral reefs 96–7, 140
creation theory 32, 49
cross-breeding 126–7

D

Darwin, Charles 29, 30–9, 40–52, 53, 55, 84, 86, 91, 101–2, 109, 129, 162
Darwin, Erasmus 40, 162
Dawkins, Richard 84–5, 91, 104, 162
Dennett, Daniel 48
detritivores/decomposers 10, 132, 134, 135
digestive systems 140, 149
dinosaurs 17, 18, 19, 20, 24–5, 29, 35, 144, 154, 155, 161
diseases, inherited 71
DNA (deoxyribonucleic acid) 64–7, 70–1, 79, 80, 85, 118, 128, 138
DNA sequencing 127–9
domestication 43, 161

E

Earth, age of the 32, 39
ecosystems 133, 134, 155, 157
environment 13, 24, 27, 33, 108
eukaryotes 130, 138–9, 160
exoskeletons 9
extinction 18–19, 35–6, 115, 119, 132, 136, 156, 157
extreme weather 25–7
eyes 8–9, 57, 58–9, 60, 63, 105–13, 118, 141

F

family resemblance 44, 53, 78, 99
fertilization 68
finches, Darwin's 38-9, 41, 45-7, 127, 160
fingers and thumbs 145
fish 115, 142, 155
FitzRoy, Robert 31
flies 7-10, 16, 28-9, 44, 56-9, 60, 62
food chains 18
fossils 34-6, 147
fungi 83, 95-6, 99, 114, 120, 127, 130, 156, 161

G

Galápagos Islands 37-9, 41, 45-7, 127, 160
gene editing 151
gene-centred view 83, 84
genes 60-73, 79-85, 91-3, 104, 127, 144-5, 150
genes, language of 66
genetic code 66
genomes 67-8, 71, 81
geology 32-3, 82
Gould, John 41

H

Hamilton, Bill 91, 162
hearts, four-chambered 143-4
Homo sapiens 103, 146-51, 157, 161
human activity 155, 156, 157
human evolution 14, 51, 102-4, 108-9, 137-51, 153
hydrothermal vents 75, 76, 77

I

ideas, evolution of 150-1
individuality 21-2
inheritance/inherited characteristics 26, 27, 44, 53-9, 69, 73, 78
insects 38, 112, 136, 161
island populations 37-9, 45-7, 127

K

kin selection 93, 98-9, 148
Kropotkin, Pyotr 86-9, 91, 94, 100, 102, 103, 162

L

Lamarck, Jean-Baptiste 40, 55-7, 162
landscapes, changing 32-3, 36, 39
language 147, 148
life
  diversity of 120-36
  extraterrestrial 152
  origins of 76-83, 130-1, 153
light detection 109, 110
Linnaeus, Carl 121-4, 162
lizards, anole 25-7, 28, 44, 53-4, 71, 161
Luca (Last Universal Common Ancestor) 130-1, 136, 161
Lyell, Charles 32-3, 36, 162

M

Malthus, Thomas 43
mammals 143-5, 154, 161
mass extinctions 18-19, 154, 156
Mendel, Gregor 59-61
meteorites 17, 19-20, 154
microbes 11-12, 68, 82, 99, 105, 127, 129, 132, 133, 138, 156
microbiomes 133, 134, 136
mitochondrion/mitochondria 130, 139
Morgan, Lilian Vaughan 58, 162
Morgan, Thomas Hunt 56-62, 127, 162
multicellular bodies 82-3, 104, 139
mutations 70-3, 78, 82-3, 97, 113, 145, 147, 150
mutual aid 89, 102
mutualism 95-7, 102
mycorrhiza 95-6, 97, 99, 114, 120

N

natural selection 21, 24-9, 40-52, 53, 56, 58, 61, 69, 71, 73, 78-9,

80, 82, 84, 87, 93, 109, 110,
112–14, 149, 152–3
Neanderthals/*Homo neanderthalensis*
147, 161
neutral mutations 71–2
niches 134–5
nucleotides 64, 65, 66

O

olfactory receptors 144–5
optic nerve 112
organs 68, 83
Origin of Species, The 50–1, 86
ostracods, giant 109
oxygen 66, 142, 143, 156

P

palaeontolgy 34–5
parasites 34, 100–1, 108
pentadactyls 142–3
phosphorus 96, 97, 99
photosynthesis 96, 97, 110
plants 12, 83, 95–6, 99, 127, 156, 161
plesiosaurs 17, 19
pollination 156
pollution 155, 158
population 21, 27, 43, 45–6, 127
Price, George 91, 162
primates 51, 145, 146, 161
proteins 66, 80, 139, 144
pterosaurs 17, 19

R

reciprocal altruism 94–5
replicators 76–83, 104, 160
reproduction 21, 42–3, 44, 60, 68,
72, 78, 85, 90, 102, 126–7, 136,
138
reptiles 17–21, 35, 128, 143–4, 161
RNA (ribonucleic acid) 64, 66, 79,
80

S

sea sponges 82, 139

sea squirts 125, 141
selective breeding 23–24, 43
selfish genes 84–5, 91, 104
sense organs 13
sensors, chemical 10
sexual reproduction 68, 70
sexual selection 118
Smith, John Maynard 91, 162
social insects 89–93
soil 11, 12, 96, 132, 156
speciation 45–7, 127–8
species
breeding ability 126
classification of 121–4
new 47, 127, 128, 132
struggle for existence 43, 45, 73, 87
sugars 96, 97, 99
survival 17, 21, 34, 44, 72, 75, 84, 85,
86, 88, 102, 113, 118–19, 134
sustainability 159
Sutton, Walter 61, 63

T

technological evolution 158
tree of life 48, 127–36, 137
trilobites 106, 112

U

urbilaterians 140
Ussher, James 32, 162

V

vampire bats 93–4, 98, 99
variations 22, 43, 44, 46, 47, 53–4,
57–61, 69–70, 73, 78, 82, 98, 113
vertebrates 107, 128, 141
viruses 64, 69, 71, 120

W

Wallace, Alfred Russel 50, 52, 162
wasps, parasitic 34, 100–1, 102
whales 15, 120, 143
wings 9, 13–14, 21, 29, 73, 150
workers, insect 89–91, 92, 98

Acknowledgements

Four books in to this new adventure, and counting! All thanks to our incredible team – a genuine example of the power of mutualism in action. Our deepest gratitude to the star players: series editor Helen Greathead, designer Alison Gadsby and commissioning editor Anthony Hinton. Sincere thanks also to copy and proof editors Julia Bruce and Philip Thomas, and to indexer Helen Peters. Working with the wider DFB team, including Fraser, Bron, Phil, Rosie, Meggie, Kate and Rachel, continues to be a joy. Thanks to David Fickling for planting the seeds that grew into this new series, and to Michael Holyoke and Liz Cross for helping nurture the emerging concept. Finally, heartfelt thanks to Dr Georg Hochberg, of the Max Planck Institute for Terrestrial Microbiology, for checking facts, allowing us to tap his deep knowledge of evolution and for his generous comments about the 'spaghetti monster'.

BM: Thanks to all my family – my kin – for their endless support, encouragement and inspiration. But especially to Cal, for inspiring this particular 'survival machine' always to think harder, empathize better and love wholeheartedly.

About the Author and Illustrator

Ben Martynoga is a biologist and writer. After a decade in the lab exploring the insides of brain cells, he swapped his white coat for a pen. Since then he has written about everything from the latest tech innovations to rewilding, running, stress, creativity, microbes and the history of science. He loves talking about science – and why it matters – with children and adults alike at science festivals, in classrooms or anywhere else. His writing appears in the *Guardian*, *New Statesman*, the *i*, the *Financial Times* and beyond. He lives, works, wanders and wonders (often all at once) in the Lake District.

Moose Allain is an artist, illustrator and prolific tweeter who lives and works in south-west England. He runs workshops and has published a book and an online guide encouraging children to draw, write and find inspiration when faced with a blank sheet of paper. Always on the lookout for interesting projects, his work has encompassed co-producing the video for the band Elbow's 'Lost Worker Bee' single and designing murals for a beauty salon in Mexico City – he's even been tempted to try his hand at stand-up comedy. His cartoons regularly feature in the UK's *Private Eye* magazine.

EXPL*O*DAPEDIA

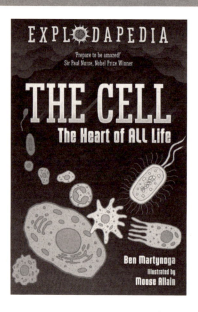

Cells are alive, and they're what life is made of.
Four billion years ago a single cell kickstarted all life on Earth. Today, your body is made up of over 30 trillion cells – every one of which is teeming with activity.

Packed with up-to-the-minute science, *The Cell* confronts the biggest mysteries of the microscopic marvels that sustain the living world. Can cells save our planet next?

'A totally fascinating book' Greg Jenner

EXPLODAPEDIA

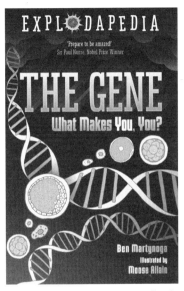

There are 40,000 genes in every cell of your body. Together, they carry all the instructions needed to make you. Nobody else has exactly the same genes as you do: you are completely unique.

Based on up-to-the-minute science, *The Gene* explores how these tiny tangles of DNA build and operate all living things. See what genes can reveal about you, and find out how today's scientists 'edit' genes. Will these breakthroughs help or harm our future?

EXPLODAPEDIA

Publishing in 2024

Rewild is a celebration of the vital role nature plays in our lives. It's a guide to reconnecting with the wild things all around us, and accepting that we humans are also part of nature. From river-nurturing wolves to climate-warrior whales and resurrected woolly mammoths, meet the creatures with the power to breathe fresh life into our fragile planet.

Ben Martynoga and Moose Allain will inspire you to see the living world in a new light and empower you to act for its future.